The Staging
Handbook

The Staging Handbook

Second Edition

FRANCIS REID

A & C Black · London

Second edition 1995
First paperback edition 1990
by A & C Black (Publishers) Limited
35 Bedford Row, London WC1R 4JH

© 1995, 1990, 1978 Francis Reid

ISBN 0–7136–4176–2

First published by Pitman Publishing Limited 1978

Second edition publishd in the USA by Heinemann
A Division of Reed Elsevier, Inc.
361 Hanover Street, Portsmouth, NH 03801–3912
Offices and Agents throughout the world.

Distributed in Canada by Reed Books Canada,
75 Clegg Road, Markham, Ontario L6G 1A1

ISBN 0–435–08682–0

CIP catalogue records for this book are
available from the British Library and the Library of Congress.

Cover photograph of the fit up for *Sleeping Beauty*
at Polka Theatre for Children, Wimbledon, London
(Designer: Bridget Kimak/Photo: John Reading)

Photoset in 10 on 12pt Raleigh by
Rowland Phototypesetting Limited,
Bury St Edmunds, Suffolk
Printed and bound in Great Britain
by The Bath Press, Bath, Avon

Contents

Acknowledgements

The author would like to express his gratitude to all those who helped by providing illustrations or allowing their work to be interrupted by the author's own camera. In particular, thanks are due to Reg Allen, The Appleton Partnership, Rudolf Biste, Alex Blyth, Bytecraft, Bill Crisp, Billy Crockett, Jeremy B. Collins, Alistair Couborough, June Dandridge, Shirley Duff Gray, Heinz Fritz, Ian Gillespie, Harman Audio, Law and Dunbar-Naysmith, Pani, Selecon, Teatro, Dorothy Tenham, Anna Welbourne, Ludo Wynn, and the unique picture archives of Strand Lighting.

Prologue

In an ideal world, the preparation of a theatre performance would be a process of gradual evolution from script to audience. The sung or spoken word would be clothed in movement and gradually all the elements – scenery, costume, props, music, sound, light – would be added. The whole process would take place on the actual stage to be used for performance and would be a delicate creative process free from the rigours of budgeted money and scheduled time: a tender blossom to be revealed to its audience when, and only when, it was judged ready by its creators.

Reality is somewhat different from such ideals: much of the creative process takes place in rehearsal rooms far removed from the stage; time and money are always short; and was any production ever considered ready by its creative team?

In preparing a theatre performance, whether amateur or professional, there are normally two distinct processes:

First, the acting rehearsals (without scenery, costumes or lights), usually carried out in a rehearsal room rather than on the stage which will house the performance, and

Secondly, the technical and dress rehearsals where this previously rehearsed acting performance is integrated with all the technical apparatus of the stage.

This second phase, the *staging*, is relatively complex, particularly within the context of the short time scale in which it has to be accomplished. It is therefore hardly surprising that many shows which looked promising in their final run-through in the rehearsal room, lose something – or even fall apart – in the transfer to the stage.

This *staging process* is largely a matter of organisation and communication, both prior to and during the technical and dress rehearsals. Effective staging depends upon team-work. Every single member of the production team, including the actors, needs to have some understanding of what each department is trying to do and where its particular problems lie.

Everyone working in theatre has a streak of idealism, a yearning for perfection, and a tendency towards single-minded pursuit of their personal speciality. Everybody, in the nicest possible way, is in it for grabs. The designer wants a lavish set, the lighting crew want a huge spotlight rig, the wardrobe people have visions of lush brocades and exquisite wigs, the sound department is convinced that success can only result from continuous multi-track birdsong and burbling brook . . . and so on. Where stands the actor in all this? Or the playwright? Or, especially, the audience?

In the theatre, as in the life which it reflects, the conversion of ideals into reality inevitably involves compromise. Success usually results from careful balancing so that one element does not get out of proportion with the others. If the balance is correct, the whole can be more than just the sum of the parts: the compromise of ideals will result in an ideal compromise.

Although much of this book is written in terms of the professional theatre, its approach to the solution of staging problems is universal – these problems are common to all forms of theatre, whether they be organised on an amateur, educational or professional basis.

Since the first edition of this book in 1978, the processes of staging have changed in matters of detail rather than in fundamentals. Budgets may seem more generous and schedules more relaxed, but a tendency to increased technical complexity requires even more tighter control of money and time.

Scenery has become more lavish, tending once again to support actors rather than leave them exposed in a masking box with a few significant objects on a raked floor. A decline in the use of natural timber, discreetly stained, has led to a revival in the art of scenic painting. Lighting control is now almost entirely by computer but the basics of lighting are unchanged: the unassailable frontier remains that light travels in straight lines and generates heat. However there have been some mechanical refinements in spotlights and a tendency for lamp wattages to rise. The simple focus spot has been reborn with a new plano-convex lens giving a clean smooth light with a soft beam edge, free from the excessive scatter associated with fresnels. An ever widening range of diffuser filters offers more precise control of beam quality. The fast plotting capability of the new desks allows lighting sessions to be shorter and balancing to be carried out during actor rehearsals – but this does mean that lighting designers must be even better prepared.

Sound has continued to be a major growth area. Constantly improving domestic standards of sound reproduction have raised audience expectation of quality to a level difficult to achieve in a theatre auditorium. Efforts to match the close presence of television sound often result in a level so loud that the words do not appear to be coming from the actors' mouths unless they adopt an impossibly broad acting style. The use of radio microphones has grown, often with every member of the cast wired for sound. But there is still a tendency for sound to be given less status, and consequently less scheduled time, than it requires.

Staffing levels have increased to cope with heavier productions, the maintenance needs of new technology, and the more flexible working patterns which acknowledge the unsocial hours which are the nature of the entertainment industry. The generic word 'technician' has come into increasing use with less rigid departmentalisation of stage staffs. 'Technical Manager' is taking over from such traditional job titles as 'resident stage manager' and 'master carpenter'. Increasingly complex productions, with bigger technical budgets to be met from a decline in total funding, have stimulated tighter management structures with the *Production Manager* in the key budgeting and scheduling role for the staging departments.

So, despite some new technology, the theatre remains a people industry where detailed organisation is the key to successful staging – just as it was when this book was first written.

Part I

ORGANISING THE STAGING

1 Organisation

Efficient staging requires efficient planning and efficient planning requires some sort of organisational structure. *Organisation* is one of the more suspect words of our times. It is something that we tend to recoil from. The word has an image of corporate inefficiency: an anonymous body whose decisions, although taken in the name of logic, appear to lack simple common-sense and humanity. But organisation (the process) carried out by an organisation (the structure) is essential for the process of making a plan and implementing it. Successful organisation is closely linked to optimum size. Undersize can result in inadequate planning producing inadequate actions. Oversize can result in the generation of paper which tends to produce more paper rather than actions. Either way, there is a loss: a loss of money and a loss of time.

ORGANISATIONAL STRUCTURE

To make and implement decisions, an organisational structure is required. There are two possibilities: a structure has to be set up or one already exists. Neither situation is entirely satisfactory. An existing organisational structure has built-in defects (often people) and these defects may be virtually irremovable. On the other hand, setting up an organisation from scratch is a daunting task and even worse deficiencies may get incorporated. The imperfect organisation that you know is probably better than the (possibly) perfect organisation that you do not know. The known is something that we can learn to live with: many deficiencies, if recognised, can be turned into advantages. It is the unknown – the blank sheet – that holds terror.

The traditional British or American theatre set-up is two-part: owners of theatres rent their buildings to producers of shows. This gives rise to an *us and them* situation where any production has two sets of people and two sets of materials: ours and theirs. Indeed, as both parties use the words 'ours' and 'theirs' with opposite meanings, it can be quite important to realise who's who during a technical rehearsal! The situation is most obvious with a theatre company moving into a London, Broadway or touring theatre, but it also arises in a village or school hall: anyone who has dealt with a caretaker, or indeed has been a caretaker, will recognise the *us and them* syndrome. The situation can arise even in theatres where the bricks and mortar are owned by the show's producer.

The producer's technical staff know the details of the show because they have been planning and rehearsing prior to moving on to the stage. They are the natural people to manage the operation, but they must *communicate*. Most people will feel involved if they know where they are heading and by what route it is proposed to travel. Every production has to have a destination and a map. This is the only way to avoid an undercurrent, from all sides, of such muttered thoughts as 'I wish they would make up their minds', 'Here we go again', or perhaps just plain 'Obstructionists!'.

DEPARTMENTS   The traditional departmental divisions are into *stage* (or *scenery*), *props*, *electrics* and *wardrobe*. There is a substantial folklore devoted to true and apocryphal tales of finely drawn demarcation lines. Electrics is fairly easy to define once it is accepted that the handling of a chandelier is traditionally the responsibilty of props when it is merely decorative, but is looked after by electrics if it actually lights up. The distinctions between scenery and props have become somewhat blurred with the growth of new styles of design and new techniques of construction. Hand props and furniture are easy to classify, and the dressings on a conventional box set may also be easily recognised as props. However some of the more representational design styles produce units which are both (some cynics would probably say neither!). This can lead to a negative definition of props as being everything which cannot be classified as scenery, wardrobe or electrics. Even this definition places a large question mark over costume props – swords, spectacles, jewellery, and the like.

As a theatre increases in size and complexity, the departments become more specialised. For example, *flys* and *sound* become separate departments rather than specialised duties of members of the stage and electrics departments respectively. *Maintenance*, which in a small theatre is looked after by the production staff, becomes a separate department. Conversely, the smaller the theatre, the more likely are its staff to be versatile technicians able and willing to deal with everything that happens backstage. In all theatres, with the exception of the very largest, there is an increasing move towards the greater flexibility of a crew of generic technicians undertaking all duties as required under the direction of specialist departmental heads. As a result of this greater flexibility, *Technician* seems likely to become the most frequently used job title.

JOB TITLES

In trying to understand the structure of any particular organisation, the actual job titles of the personnel can be somewhat confusing. *Technical Director*, for example, has been known to cover everything from the executive at the top of a huge organisational pyramid to a jack-of-all trades who builds the scenery, stokes the boilers, and works the lighting control with one hand while flying the house-tabs with the other. Status adjectives like *director, manager, chief, supervisor*, and *master* are liberally bestowed in the theatre, frequently with qualifying adjectives like *general*. Apart from such terminology being in line with the larger than life ballyhoo which is an essential part of theatre, it is not unknown for an inflated job title to be offered in compensation for an inadequate salary increase.

Some of the job titles, with an indication of some of their varying functions, are:

Producer

Formerly the person who directed the actors. Now the *packager* of a production: the person who brings together script, theatre, director, designers, possibly the star(s), but above all the money.

Director

Has the ultimate responsibility for the production's overall concept and that concept's realisation. Controls the actors directly and controls everything else indirectly through the other members of the production team (scene, costume and lighting designers, stage manager, etc.). Must have ultimate veto, but should rarely be seen using it.

Designer

Responsible for the conception of all the visual elements and the supervision of their execution within an agreed budget. Where scenery, props or costumes are made specially, supplies a design. Where anything is to be rented or borrowed, is responsible for the choice. Separate designers may be employed for scenery and costumes.

Lighting Designer

Conceives the lighting style in consultation with the director and the rest of the design team, plans an appropriate equipment rig (within the budget) and supervises its installation and focusing. Composes the balance of the lighting at the lighting rehearsals and supervises its execution and modification throughout the technical and dress rehearsals.

Technical Director (Administrator/ Manager)

Co-ordinates and budgets the work of all technical production departments. Essential in a large organisation with several productions simultaneously in performance and rehearsal.

Production Manager

In a big organisation responsible for the technical preparation of new productions from first idea to first performance, co-ordinating the operations and budgets of the organisation's own workshops and/or outside contractors and suppliers. In a small organisation, may also be senior stage manager and/or technician.

Stage Director Formerly the title of the senior member of the stage management team but abandoned when producers began to be called directors.

Stage Manager (SM) In overall control of the performance and responsible for signalling the cues that co-ordinate the work of the actors and technicians. In the absence of the director (or an appointed deputy), the stage manager is responsible for ensuring that the production as a whole, including individual acting performances, does not make any substantial departure from the original.

Deputy Stage Manager In British theatre, 'runs' the show from the prompt corner (giving the cues, calling and prompting the artists) to leave the stage manager free to supervise the entire stage area and/or check out the performance from the auditorium.

Assistant Stage Managers (ASMs) In addition to giving general assistance to the stage manager and deputy, and understudying their functions in cueing the performance, the ASMs may have responsibility for such departments as props and sound. In general the smaller the organisation, the more the ASMs have to 'do' rather than merely supervise.

Company Manager The producer frequently does not own the theatre where the show is being performed. The company manager is then the producer's senior representative in the theatre, liaising with the theatre management, and usually responsible for preparation of day-to-day accounts including salary payments to the company. Thus the company manager is the administrative line of communication between the producer and both the theatre management and the acting company. In Britain, particularly in London and on tour, the job is often combined with the duties of stage manager.

Heads of Departments (HODs) Usually used to denote the theatre's resident staff (particularly master carpenter and chief electrician) rather than the producing company's staff.

Dayman Traditional title, increasingly being replaced by 'technician', for a member of the stage staff (*stage dayman*) or electrics staff (*electrics dayman*) employed on a permanent full-time basis. Often classified as *first dayman* or *second dayman* according to seniority and experience.

Showman A part-time member of the stage, props or electrics staff employed, usually on a casual basis, for performances only.

Master Carpenter	The senior member of the stage staff. Responsible, through management of the stage crew, for the correct and safe movement of all scenery during rehearsals and performances. Normally also responsible for the general organisation of everything in the backstage area except electrics, but including maintenance, cleanliness, safety and fire precautions.
Chief Machinist	An alternative name for master carpenter, particularly in larger theatres or opera houses with mechanised stages.
Mechanists	Alternative (particularly in Australasia) for scenery handling staff.
Flyman	Supervises all flying of scenery above the stage. Normally a senior assistant of the master carpenter. Only in the biggest theatres are the duties confined to flying.
Property Master	Senior member of the property staff. Organises the handling of props at performances. In small theatres and on small tours, this organisation of props may be in the hands of an assistant stage manager. In some production theatres, the property master may make props in addition to dealing with performances, although in the larger theatres and opera houses there is usually a separate property-making workshop staff. The property master is often a property mistress and the title property manager is coming into use.
Props	Members of the property department are often referred to as just 'props' rather than 'prop man' or other similarly formal titles.
Chief Electrician	Senior member of the electrics department. In smaller theatres, responsible for all the electrical maintenance of the building in addition to the stage lighting. In larger theatres, deals only with the stage lighting while maintenance is handled by a house engineer. In America, called *master electrician*.
Deputy Chief Electrician Assistant Chief Electrician	Self-explanatory. One of these is usually the operator of the lighting control 'board'. In theatres with no separate sound department, another deputy or assistant assumes responsibility for sound.
Stage Electrics	Rank and file electricians who plug up equipment during scene changes, handle microphones, etc. Often part-time show crew.
Limes	Often used to describe follow spot operators.
Sound	Is still at such a relatively young point in its growth as a separate department that job titles have not yet settled into any uniformity. The

terms sound engineer, operator, technician, consultant, supervisor are in common but not standard use.

Resident Stage Manager

In many theatres there is a traditionally uneasy truce between the master carpenter and the chief electrician: both are responsible to the theatre manager for their respective departments, but neither is in charge of the whole stage operation. In most touring theatres, the master carpenter is designated *resident stage manager* and is in overall charge of the stage, being responsible to the theatre manager for the staff and building, and to the touring company manager for the performance facilities. When there is no touring stage manager (as, for example, when the theatre is playing variety), the resident stage manager assumes all stage management duties and responsibilities. There is a trend for the title of *Technical Manager* to replace that of Resident Stage Manager.

Wardrobe Mistress/ Master/Manager/ Supervisor

The senior person in charge of costumes. The wardrobe department has two main functions: the *making* of costumes during the production period and the *maintenance* of these costumes during the run of performances. The making may be done by outside contractors and/or in the theatre's own workshops. Producers often employ a *costume supervisor* to co-ordinate the making and buying of clothes for a production. *Wardrobe manager* is a title increasingly used in the larger organisations where the senior wardrobe person has to supervise extensive costume making workshops. In this case the title *wardrobe maintenance* is often used for the day-to-day repairing, laundry and organisation of costumes between and during performances.

Wig Master/ Mistress or Perruquier

In theatres with a classical or operatic repertoire, the number of wigs requires a special department with its own departmental head.

Dressers

Members of the wardrobe performance staff (often part-time) who help individual actors with care and changing of their costumes.

Hallkeeper

The formal title for the stage doorkeeper. Responsible for the security of the backstage area, screening visitors, looking after keys, mail, messages, etc. Titles which include the word 'security' are coming into fashion.

Housekeeper

Supervises the cleaning staff for the entire theatre including dressing rooms and backstage areas, with the exception of the actual stage and workshops which are usually cleaned by the staff of the appropriate staging departments.

This list of job titles does not pretend to be exhaustive or absolutely accurate, especially in what might be called the 'small print'. Many holders of these titles may even deny that their duties are as described! It is only intended to give a basic idea of broad general usage. Later chapters on individual departments discuss jobs in more detail.

2   Types of Organisation

Before discussing some typical organisations, we should look at theatre's great divide: 'production' and 'running'. The climax of staging is the first performance. Events prior to this are referred to as *production* and the expenses incurred are *production costs*. As the rehearsal period produces no income, these production costs are in the nature of an investment. The first performance is the start of the *run* and the expenses are *running costs*. The sale of seats now produces an income which has to cover not just the running costs but a proportion of the production costs equivalent to at least the total of these production costs divided by the number of performance weeks. Additionally, if the capital finance for the production costs has been raised by commercial means, the income will be required to produce a profit at a rate reflecting the high risk nature of the investment. Box office income, even from a full house, is frequently inadequate to cover the costs of a performance – particularly the production costs but often the running costs also. The question of augmenting income with subsidy is discussed in the next chapter.

But the matter of costs and their budgeting is only one aspect of the divide between the production and running periods. The personnel required will vary not just in numbers but in degree of specialisation and in personality. There can be a tendency among technical staff to find the production period much more exciting than the performances and this is understandable, particularly in the case of a play with a permanent set and few cues. But the performance is, and must be, the climax. Not just the first performance but every performance. The 'system' often favours production staffs in terms of status and salary, but the theatre has at least equal need of the technician whose speciality is to contribute to the meticulous running of the ninety-ninth performance.

PRODUCERS WITHOUT THEATRES

Production organisations can be surprisingly small in terms of both staff and hardware. London producers, eminently successful financially and artistically, have been known to operate from a pair of small offices

'The Mousetrap' – every producer's dream – the show with an apparently endless run and no scene changes.

housing the producer, a production manager, a business manager and a secretary.

The function of such a producer is to bring together the best possible team to realise a particular script. Starting with a mutually compatible director and star(s), the producer, with their approval, goes on to select key production personnel from the freelance pool. Where possible, this production team is assembled from those whose sympathies and experience seem appropriate and who seem likely to be able to work together, often because they have done so successfully in the past. With a theatre of appropriate size, type and location in mind, the whole package is budgeted to present an investment attraction in the traditional theatrical mould of potential high profit at certain high risk. As rising costs force theatrical financing away from private investment towards public subsidy, the financing becomes a matter of budgeting for a certain but calculated and restricted loss. Each production is virtually an independent company with its accountancy simplified by negotiating with contractors to buy production-cost hardware such as scenery and costumes, and to rent running-cost hardware such as lighting equipment, sound equipment and perhaps props.

NON-PRODUCING
THEATRES

Non-producing theatres, sometimes called receiving theatres, require the smallest staffs. All construction takes place in outside contractors' workshops and is brought to the theatre as a ready-to-assemble package. Extra casual staff can be hired to augment the theatre's small stage crew, and for the first fit-up at least one of the workshop carpenters will be present. For subsequent moves to other theatres, the fit-up will be supervised by a touring carpenter. Many contemporary design styles for plays require few, if any, scene changes during the performance. Where changes are necessary, they tend to be confined to flying or other re-arrangement of scenic elements within a permanent framework.

Such a theatre might have a resident staff of no more than six: a master carpenter and a chief electrician, each with two assistants. The carpenter's assistants double as property master and flyman respectively, with one of the electricians taking care of sound. However, in such a set-up there is a considerable degree of overlap between duties as days off tend to reduce the number of available staff in the theatre to five or even four. When necessary, the staff is augmented for performances by show crew who are normally part-timers following another occupation by day.

Musicals require a larger staff but in a non-producing theatre this is mainly a performance requirement met by a large show crew, although there is also likely to be a slightly larger permanent day staff because musicals are performed in larger theatres where more staff are required for maintenance.

Non-producing theatres present 'runs' of shows: either the short fixed one- or two-week runs of the touring system, or the open-ended runs of the West End or Broadway where it is hoped that every show will run as long as 'The Mousetrap'. Runs have labour-intensive peaks – get-ins, performances and get-outs – with relative quiet in between. The system of part-time casual show staff is the only economic way to deal with these peaks of activity, and indeed some of the most dedicated and skilled technicians are to be found among the part-timers of the regional touring theatres.

**PRODUCING
THEATRES**

The work pattern of a producing theatre is rather different. The labour requirement is more evenly distributed, with fewer peaks of labour-intensive activity. There are three basic ways in which the performances can be organised: repertory, repertoire, stagione.

In *repertory*, the production has a run of limited length, and planning normally requires that the length of this run be decided before the opening night. At any given time there is usually one production in performance, another in rehearsal, and several in varying degrees of planning. At the conclusion of the run of performances, the scenic

The West Yorkshire Playhouse in Leeds is a major regional producing repertory theatre, housed in a complex which includes comprehensive audience facilities and all the necessary workshops for scenery, prop and costume construction. The contrasting formats of its two auditoria allow productions to be staged in a wide range of styles. (Architects: The Appleton Partnership.)

The Courtyard Theatre.

The Quarry Theatre.

hardware is normally dispersed with re-usable items being returned to stock.

In *repertoire*, several productions are available for performance during any particular period. Several performances of the same production may be given on adjacent days or there may be a changeover every single day with perhaps a gap of up to a couple of weeks between two performances of a particular work. This latter situation often arises in opera houses, particularly where, as in Germany, many of the seats are sold on seasonal subscriptions. These may guarantee that by attending on, for example, every alternate Tuesday, a subscriber will see the entire season's repertoire of opera, ballet and drama. Or the first Thursday in each month may bring a cycle of contemporary opera. Thus, in any given short period, several productions may be in performance and several more in active rehearsal. At the end of a season, the newer sets, props, costumes, etc., are usually stored complete for future revival.

Stagione is rather like repertoire except that, at any given time, a very small range of productions is in performance. A production is given intensive rehearsals, followed by a burst of performances close together, then placed in store. Each revival is rehearsed, often with major cast changes, almost as if it were a new production. Under the stagione system, there are fewer productions in performance and rehearsal with resultant simplification of most organisational matters, particularly casting and technical stage changeovers. It is hardly surprising that a higher standard of performance becomes possible. In opera, where each performance involves certain financial loss even in a capacity house, an extreme form of stagione is sometimes operated where only one opera

The three auditoria of the Royal National Theatre in London operate the modified repertoire system known as *Stagione*.

20 JAN–11 MAR		OLIVIER		LYTTELTON		COTTESLOE	
Friday	20	January	† 7.15 The Merry Wives of Windsor	7.30	The Children's Hour	7.30	Alice's Adventures... **P**
Saturday	21	January		2.15	The Children's Hour	2.30	Alice's Adventures...
			† 7.15 The Merry Wives of Windsor	7.30	The Children's Hour	7.30	Alice's Adventures...
Monday	23	January	† 7.15 The Merry Wives of Windsor	7.30	Broken Glass	7.30	Alice's Adventures...
Tuesday	24	January	† 2.00 The Merry Wives of Windsor	2.15	Broken Glass	2.30	Alice's Adventures...
			† 7.15 The Merry Wives of Windsor	7.30	Broken Glass	7.30	Alice's Adventures...
Wednesday	25	January					
			† 7.15 The Merry Wives of Windsor	7.30	Broken Glass **P**	7.30	Two Weeks...Queen
Thursday	26	January				2.30	Two Weeks...Queen
			● 7.00 The Merry Wives of Windsor	7.30	Out of a house...	7.30	Two Weeks...Queen
Friday	27	January				2.30	Two Weeks...Queen
			7.15 The Merry Wives of Windsor **P**	7.30	Out of a house...	7.30	Two Weeks...Queen
Saturday	28	January	2.00 The Merry Wives of Windsor	2.15	Out of a house...	2.30	Two Weeks...Queen
			7.15 The Merry Wives of Windsor	7.30	Out of a house...	7.30	Two Weeks...Queen
Monday	30	January	7.15 The Merry Wives of Windsor	7.30	Out of a house...		NO PERFORMANCE
Tuesday	31	January	7.15 The Wind in the Willows	7.30	Broken Glass		NO PERFORMANCE
Wednesday	1	February	2.00 The Wind in the Willows				NO PERFORMANCE
			7.15 The Wind in the Willows	7.30	Broken Glass		
Thursday	2	February		2.15	Broken Glass		
			7.15 The Wind in the Willows	7.30	Broken Glass	† 7.30	Dealer's Choice
Friday	3	February	S 7.15 The Wind in the Willows	7.30	The Children's Hour	† 7.30	Dealer's Choice
Saturday	4	February	2.00 The Wind in the Willows	2.15	The Children's Hour	† 2.30	Dealer's Choice
			7.15 The Wind in the Willows	7.30	The Children's Hour	† 7.30	Dealer's Choice

The Quarry Theatre.
Typical programme of
a German opera
house with an
extensive repertoire.

BERLIN,
KOMISCHE OPER
  1 Giulio Cesare
  2 Figaro
  3 Gewaltige Hahnrei
  4 Orfeo ed Euridice
  5 Brigands
 10 Cav/Pag
 11 Trittico
 13, 14 Carmen
 15 Traviata
 17 Hoffmann
 18 Figaro
 19 Zauberflöte
 20 Cenerentola
 21 Holländer
 22 Entführung
 24, 25 Tale of Tsar Saltan
 26 Rienzi
 27 Giulio Cesare
 28 Traviata
 30 Zauberflöte

April
  1 Gewaltige Hahnrei
  2, 4 Hoffmann
  5 Figaro
  7 Bohème
  8 Giulio Cesare

is performed at a time and the theatre remains closed on evenings between these performances. This eliminates many of the costs and technical complications of daily changeovers.

Until recently, most producing theatres preferred to have all construction work carried out in their own workshops rather than by contractors. In repertory, where the productions are mounted for short runs and there are no daily changeovers, the stage and props staff can be available for some daytime construction work. The pressures of repertoire, on the other hand, normally require a completely different workshop staff to be employed. Because of the inevitable peaks and troughs in the flow of work through a theatre's workshop, outside contractors are easier to budget on a production-by-production basis and are normally more cost effective in the longer term. Either way, producing theatres require much bigger staffs and an altogether more complex organisation to bring the various staging elements together in the right place and time – and at the right cost.

3 Budgeting and Scheduling

The key words in the organisation of successful staging are *budgeting* and *scheduling*: the management of money and the management of time. To strive towards minimum expenditure of both is a right and proper objective, but it is not enough. Minimum is not necessarily optimum: success is getting the correct *balance* between the many different ingredients in the staging mix.

Budgeting and scheduling are essentially the *proportioning* of money and time. The documents produced by this process – the budgets and the schedules – have two functions. They are a means of working towards staging decisions, and they are a means of communicating these decisions.

BUDGETING

Theatre financing has always been precarious: although many fortunes have been made, very many more have been lost. To the economist, a theatre performance is a labour-intensive, short-life product with an unpredictable sales volume from a grossly under-used prime retail site.

The larger forms of theatre, particularly opera, have always required a deficit-budgeting approach: without even considering the material costs, the number of people involved is such that the box-office income from a full house cannot cover the salaries. It is, of course, possible to raise seat prices towards economically realistic levels, but, as seat prices rise, there is a proportionate fall in the number sold. In any case, contemporary society has accepted that there should be some attempt to make the performing arts available to all income groups.

Apart from the hit Broadway or West-End musical (and there are many more flops than hits!), it is now virtually impossible to produce any form of theatre without subsidy. The last apparently unsubsidised theatre is the comedy or whodunit with a cast no larger than half-a-dozen and no change of scene. Or a mega-marketed musical, full of visual effects and with a recording-hyped score, preferably by Andrew Lloyd–Webber. Even apparently 'profitable' productions usually have some hidden form of subsidy. A 'try-out' in a subsidised regional theatre may have reduced the risk of failure and may even have met some of the production costs, the theatre building is available for rent at less than its true market figure because planning regulations prevent its redevelopment, and many actors and technicians provide a hidden subsidy by working, through love of the theatre, for less financial reward than would be regarded as adequate in other walks of life.

Thus most theatre operations have two sources of income: *earned* and *awarded*, corresponding to *box-office* and *subsidy* from public funds or commercial sponsors. The danger is that there seems to be something of a psychological divide. As soon as a theatre starts to receive subsidised income, there can be a temptation for financial control to become a little less stringent, a little less urgent; for ideals to be pursued with an ever decreasing consideration for cost. Throughout life, ideals have to be tempered with reality and theatre is no different.

Indeed, restrictions often provide the very stimulus for successful creative activity – often, but not always. We are back to our basic quest for that *optimum* which, in financial terms as in everything else, is rarely the maximum or the minimum. There is a hoary old management joke reply to the request for additional production finance: 'Shall I see it from the box office?' This is still valid if we transform the old literal meaning of 'Will it bring people into the theatre?' to 'Will it help the audience to understand and enjoy the play?'

A staging budget has two components: production costs and running costs. As already noted, the production costs include all expenditure incurred up to the first night, while the running costs are the performance expenses. Production costs and running costs interact. Sometimes an increase in production cost will cause an increase in running cost, sometimes a decrease. For example, more elaborate scenery may require extra crew to handle it during performance. On the other hand, production expenditure on mechanisation may reduce the number of performance crew.

It is not enough for a budget to be realistic: it must be *agreed* to be realistic by all those who have to operate within it. It should not be the secret document that it nearly always is. Unfortunately it is very common for each department to be told only their own maximum figure: there is no communication of the total sum allowed for a production, nor of the inter-departmental breakdown. In an activity so dependent on team-work, there just has to be more corporate decision making – although there will normally be a point where the person carrying the financial responsibility (often the production manager with the backing of the theatre director) will have to decree 'Enough discussion, enough, this is what we are going to agree!' Each department can then go off, knowing how they fit in to the general scheme and being in a position to say 'I told you so' at a later date. Budgets have to be progressed and reviewed at frequent intervals during the production period. Requirements change and develop during rehearsals and so it is wise to include a substantial contingency amount in the total figure.

The budgeting of staging costs varies between types of theatre. Producers without their own theatres will have to cost every single item of the production. However, as they will almost certainly deal with a relatively small number of contractors, the budgeting will be in largish block sums. For example, having established a total contract price for the scenery construction, the detailed costing of labour and materials becomes the contractor's worry. Similarly the lighting contractor's price will include the difficult-to-predict cost of blown-lamp replacement. Naturally, the contractor's figures are high to allow a margin for miscalculation, but producers know exactly where they stand and budgeting is reduced to block figures, with fewer imponderables and less need for large contingency allowances. The contractors have taken over some of the risk.

In a producing theatre with its own workshop facilities, budgeting often becomes detailed cost control of materials. The labour content is usually salaried and at a fixed cost – its economical use therefore becomes a matter for scheduling rather than budgeting. If the work cannot be done by scheduling existing labour, then a decision must be taken in terms of the available options: overtime, temporary additional staff, part use of contractors, or simplified staging.

Every theatre organisation is different and whether these differences are fundamental or more subtle, each organisation needs its own detailed individual budgeting approach – but there are certain common hazards to be borne in mind:

- There are only certain areas where cost control can be exercised. For example, in a Mozart opera you cannot cut the second bassoon but there is a possibility of economising on the wigs. (Although there are people, including not just wig-specialists but even some directors, who would cheerfully eliminate half the orchestra rather than have one chorus hair less than perfect!)
- As the opening performance approaches, there is an atmosphere of mounting hysteria where money becomes irrelevant in the minds of those whose life has become temporarily but totally obsessed by the horizons of the production. Production managers cannot remain completely cool and detached through this phase (if they do, they are likely to have a less than ideal temperament for dealing with theatre people) but they must remain cool enough to restrict last-minute financial hysteria to a sensible spending of any remains of the contingency allowance in the original budget.
- There is a psychological barrier at the point where a theatre becomes dependent on subsidy rather than box-office income alone. As soon as this barrier is broken through, there is a

tendency for budget thinking to move from 'How much can we afford to spend?' to 'How much do we need to spend?' Artistically this may be a much more desirable situation: but how do we define 'need'?

- In general, theatre people are not very good with figures. Their estimates are produced in a spirit of optimism. It is surely better to go for a pessimistic estimate: there is no greater pleasure than achieving an artistic success, and doing it under budget.

SCHEDULING

In theatre, there is no such thing as late delivery of the finished product. The customers (audience) have contracts (tickets) and, at the appointed hour on the appointed day, they come to collect the product (performance) in person. Therefore, the first scheduling decision must be to determine the day of the opening performance. There are strong economic pressures to have this as early as possible. A theatre without performances (known as a *dark* theatre) is a very expensive place. But a theatre to which no one comes because the performances are under-rehearsed is even more expensive. Artistic pressures to delay the opening as long as possible counter the economic pressures to open as soon as possible. This indicates the compromise: open as soon as is feasible without prejudicing the quality of the production. This is a decision that requires rather fine judgement, made even more difficult by the need to decide a long time in advance – usually before rehearsals have even commenced.

Another key date is the beginning of the technical fit-up on stage. This date varies according to the type of theatre. In a repertoire theatre, the technical and dress rehearsals must be slotted into the performance schedule of current productions. In this case, the staging period will probably extend over at least a couple of weeks and the early technical rehearsals may be carried out with some of the settings, props, wardrobe, and lighting unfinished.

The more common case – especially in British and American theatre, both professional and amateur – is the 'run' where only one production is in performance at any given time. From the moment of getting into the theatre, the stage is totally committed to the preparation of the new production. The fundamental staging period to be scheduled is therefore the time available between the get-in and the opening performance. Naturally, for this staging period to work efficiently, the time leading up to the get-in has to be carefully scheduled so that every possible preparation is completed in readiness for the moment of gaining access to the stage.

Scheduling, therefore, involves two countdowns: first, to the get-in and, secondly, to the performance. The countdown to the get-in is probably simpler: to a large extent, individual departments are working on their own. The need is to ensure that each department reaches a state of maximum preparedness by the big day. The countdown between get-in and first performance depends on integration. Apart from completing any individual departmental work that is only possible on the stage, the principal need is the co-ordination of departments. Certain things must be done in the correct sequence, or rather, overlapping sequence.

The scientific approach to scheduling would be by critical path analysis, with its attendant bar charts, pert charts and supporting jargon. However a sensitivity for theatre and an aptitude for critical paths are rarely found within the same person. Satisfactory scheduling can be accomplished by more empirical methods where decisions are made on the basis of experience plus just a touch of that creative guesswork which has to be the basis of so many decisions in areas as subjective as the performing arts.

Some of the details of scheduling will be discussed later in the context of the problems of the different stage departments and the different types of production. Meanwhile a few of the commoner hazards may be listed:

- Schedules are not imposed: they are agreed. A successful schedule must not only be realistic, it must be *agreed* by all participants to be realistic – even if agreement has been reached, as it will be, with some reluctance.
- It is rarely possible (no, let's face it – never possible) to allocate enough time to meet the ideal requirements of each of the staging departments. In place of the ideal of 'What do we want to achieve?', the approach often has to become 'What do we have time to achieve?'.
- Whereas it may be a justifiable risk to hope that five hours' work can be squeezed into four by special effort, it is improvident to plan to compress eight into four.
- Individual theatre people vary in their ability to estimate time: their estimates are often excessively optimistic or excessively pessimistic.
- Forget such conventional showbiz rhubarb as 'It'll be all right on the night' or 'A bad dress rehearsal means a good first night'.

Part II

THE STAGING DEPARTMENTS

4 Stage Management

The stage management team co-ordinate the work of all the staging departments: and if any of these departments does not exist in a particular production set-up, then the stage management also carry out the duties of that missing department. Thus, in an ideal world, the stage management would only have to manage. But in reality, they often have to 'do' as well.

The functions and duties of stage management fall into four main periods: rehearsal room, fit-up, stage rehearsals and performance.

REHEARSAL ROOM

Rehearsal room activities are not strictly the concern of this book, but the stage management's organisational functions at this point may be summarised as:

Scheduling rehearsals

The stage manager (SM) assists the director to devise a logical working schedule which makes the best use of the actors' time, giving due regard to contracts, union agreements and humanity. In accordance with this schedule, the SM is then responsible for:

- Booking suitable rehearsal rooms.
- Calling artists (i.e. notifying them of time, place and probable duration of each rehearsal).
- Calling rehearsal pianists for musical shows.
- Arranging costume fittings and informing artists, costumiers and designers of these arrangements.
- Liaising with specialist departments such as lighting and sound about suitable times when they can see run-throughs.

Running rehearsals

- Marking out the rehearsal room floor to indicate the geography of the scenery, and obtaining such substitute furniture and properties as may be necessary for rehearsal purposes.
- Recording the 'moves' in the prompt copy and constantly updating it to include the continuous changes that are an inevitable part of the rehearsal process.

- Prompting tactfully, but with increasingly detailed firmness as rehearsals develop.
- Noting significant features of the evolving production and informing other staging departments – especially props.
- Keeping the director in touch with the hard realistic facts of the agreed set, costumes and props that are now being built and for which there is neither time nor money to transform into the scenic fantasies that are blossoming with the development of the actors' characterisations.
- Divining the moment when director and cast will require support from the tea and coffee pots – and producing such refreshment dead on cue.
- Providing a shoulder for director and cast to cry on.

GETTING IN AND FITTING UP

If the production has a complete set of competent departmental heads for scenery, lighting, sound, props, etc., the stage management team will need only to co-ordinate these departmental heads who will then supervise the work of their staffs. The success of this co-ordination depends primarily on pre-planning. In particular, on the achievement, prior to getting into the theatre, of an agreed realistic schedule. But, however good the schedule, the deadening hand of *unforeseen circumstances* will be omnipresent and the SM will have to chair many an impromptu inter-departmental meeting to revise a slipping schedule.

In particularly large organisational set-ups with production manager and/or technical director, the stage management will have only a watching brief during the fit-up – keeping a particular eye on the interests of the director and actors who tend to be forgotten at this intensive and critical point in the technical proceedings.

In the smallest organisations, a stage manager, of course, not only organises but 'does': and to organise the total job while actually doing part of it is much more difficult than standing aside and taking a calculated view of the total proceedings.

In a medium-sized operation the areas which particularly require SM-assisted decision-making include 'deading the borders': deciding on an optimum height for the masking borders to satisfy the often conflicting ideals of the designer, master carpenter and lighting designer. The department which most frequently needs assistance from the stage management in the early days is props – particularly the unpacking and setting out of the hand props which have been in use during the final days in the rehearsal room.

DEMARCATION

A stage manager in an amateur or small professional theatre does not have to worry about demarcation between the main departments of scenery, props and electrics. Fortunately, in most larger theatres, the divisions are friendly and elastic although there is a certain amount of good-natured banter between departments. Critical areas include the orchestra pit – there are some theatres where the stage crew provide the rostra for the conductor and drummer, the props supply chairs and the electrics plug up the music stands. The quick-change room is another area open for integration: the carpenter provides a couple of old flats, the props a table, mirror and chair, and the electrics a light. All this – and moving pianos – is an area where stage managers have traditionally needed to exercise their characteristic organisational tact. Demarcation sensitivities, however, are disappearing with the current move towards integrated crews of flexible multi-skilled technicians.

THE STAGE MANAGEMENT TEAM

A very small-scale show can be stage managed by two people – but never less because it is essential for the senior stage manager to be covered by an understudy. Most productions in the British theatre have a team of at least three. The *stage manager* (SM) in charge and as far as possible free from specific performance tasks. A *deputy stage manager* (DSM) who actually runs the show and gives the cues to all departments. And at least one *assistant stage manager* (ASM). The number of ASMs depends upon the size and type of show. Often there will be just one whose main occupation, at least in rehearsals and early performances, will be to supervise props. On big shows, it is often advisable to have an ASM in charge of each side of the stage, and small plays usually include the working of taped sound effects in ASM duties. Touring generally requires a largish and competent stage management team, as they have to take a different theatre staff through the show every Monday night without rehearsal.

In some respects, the stage management team are like commissioned officers in the armed services: an ASM passes instructions to a master carpenter in the way that a subaltern commands a regimental sergeant major. Although the ASM would appear above the master carpenter in an organisational tree chart, it is a position that has to be secured and maintained by the exercise of what can only be called personality.

COMPANY MANAGEMENT

In British practice, the senior member of the stage management team often combines the duties of company manager and carries responsibility for the day-to-day financial affairs of the production, including payment of salaries. The actual duties of company manager vary with the type of production company presenting the show, but essentially a company manager is the link between head office and the cast and staff of the production.

ACTING STAGE MANAGERS	There was a tradition for many years that the junior members of the stage management team were people with acting rather than technical ambitions. Apart from some situations where ASMs are engaged for their understudying abilities, the practice has virtually died out. This is probably a good thing for the professional status of stage management, but perhaps not so good for young actors for whom a period of stage management at the beginning of their careers provided a useful priming in wider theatre problems. Certainly, any young ASM would be well advised to grab at any chance of 'walking on' in the occasional small part: this is very useful in gaining an understanding of the actor's problems.
ALLOCATING DRESSING ROOMS	A sensitive area and a duty that can normally be performed satisfactorily only if the stage manager knows the actors' 'pecking order' as represented by the salaries – or has become expert in divining the precise nuances of actor billing. But at least the professional has some facts to go by: there have been amateur theatre companies where less tangible features such as local community prestige and committee seniority have been known to be involved. The real problems arise when a minor character has many complex costume changes and there is only one decent room close to the stage. If it is a case of the male star making way for a lady, then an appeal to gallantry usually produces results. The other way round is not so easy: perhaps a tactful reminder of gender equality is required. Either way, blessed is the stage manager who has a theatre with only two communal dressing rooms.
LIGHTING REHEARSALS	Organisation of lighting rehearsals is discussed in later chapters, but it must be emphasised that this is a moment when it is advisable for the stage manager and deputy to be present, giving their full attention to the proceedings. It is only by involvement in this phase of the lighting that they will fully understand the reasoning behind the cues and be able to cope, in the later absence of director and lighting designer, with such problems as the re-setting of knocked spotlights.
TECHNICAL REHEARSAL	The first stage rehearsal has various names – it is usually called *The Tech* but can be called a tech-dress, a stagger-through, a stopping-dress, etc. Whatever it is called, the intention is to sort our technical problems as they affect both actor and technicians (and musicians if any). This involves a lot of stopping. Apart from technical matters like scene changes or complex cues for light and sound, it will be the first time that actors have had to deal with such things as doors and windows. The Stage Manager must be in absolute command of the stage end of

rehearsals. Although it will often be the director who shouts 'stop!', it must always be the SM who gives the word to restart. And only after all departments have been informed of which cue-state the rehearsal is picking up from, and have reported back that they are ready. Some departments may need time to go back – for example, sound may need to re-wind tapes. If a scene change goes wrong, it must be the SM who decides whether it is necessary to do it again or whether a 'talk-through' has solved the problems.

And it is the SM who must ensure that the director and actors do not let the tech slip into a change-the-production session. If there are complex production moves to be revised, and these do not affect the technical cues, then it is a matter for notes and perhaps back to the rehearsal room tomorrow while the technicians have access to the stage to clean up *their* problems.

If the show is very simple, the length of the tech rehearsal may be reduced by 'topping and tailing'. That is, chunks of dialogue and action can be cut out when such sections of the show do not involve cues. However, this is only worthwhile if the sections are quite lengthy. Otherwise the process of stopping and restarting often takes longer than letting the rehearsal run on. Moreover, the actors lose an opportunity for familiarisation and it may well be that a top-and-tailed section includes an actor traffic problem that could halt later dress rehearsals.

By the end of the tech, everyone should know what is supposed to happen and have it plotted.

DRESS REHEARSALS

It is only in a continuous non-stopping dress rehearsal that it can finally be discovered whether what is supposed to happen is actually possible. In some cases, it is the times between cues, rather than the cues themselves, that provide the limiting factor. At a dress rehearsal, stops should only be made if disaster occurs – and the restart must be from a point well before the point of disaster. At dress rehearsals, the stage management will perform their duties as in performance: the SM is in complete charge. The director's function is to keep silent and take notes.

GIVING CUES

The traditional method of giving cues was by cue light: a red signal for stand-by and a green for go. In busy musical shows, buzzers were often used as an alternative to greens for flys and electrics who found it physically difficult to stand by while concentrating on a cue light. But it is easiest for all departments to work on verbal cues: so for any size of professional show it has become standard practice for the DSM to give all cues by voice over an open sound system. The system is open in the sense that all departments hear each other's cues. This leads to a fuller

A senior member of the stage management team (the Deputy Stage Manager in the UK) integrates all aspects of the performance by calling the cues from the prompt desk. To support the restricted diagonal view of the stage from the prompt corner, one video monitor gives a frontal picture of the stage while the other relays the musical director's beat.

understanding of the whole show and the picking up of a rhythm between, for example, flys and electrics in a dissolve through a gauze.

It is important that, in calling these cues, the DSM says the operative word GO as the last word in the instructional sentence i.e. 'Flys cue 25 (pause) GO'. With 'Go flys cue 25 please' it is difficult to know the precise moment of action. Also, the beginning of the sentence provides a second stand-by on which the crew, particularly flys, normally tension their muscles.

The usefulness of the hand cue should not be overlooked when a stage manager is close to the technician being cued – this is often the case with house tabs for example. The convention is to raise the hand for stand-by and drop with a fast sweeping motion for go.

PROMPT BOOK

There are many ways of marking up a prompt copy including the use of coloured pencils for each department's cues. Here is one method of marking but it indicates the range of information that has to be recorded.

The stage management bible is the prompt book. It has two functions: firstly to form a complete record of the production and secondly to provide a running reference point for giving the cues in performance. Since the cues (usually written as Q) have to be read in what might be described as 'real time', prominence is given to them, often by the use of coloured pencils. A prompt copy is normally made by interleaving the text pages with blank pages in a ring binder. In very complex musical shows, there can be so many cues that it is difficult to cope with a traditional prompt copy during performance and it may be simpler to use a sequence cue sheet. It is essential that the prompt copy be easy to read by all members of the SM team and kept safely in the theatre overnight (but not left in the prompt corner).

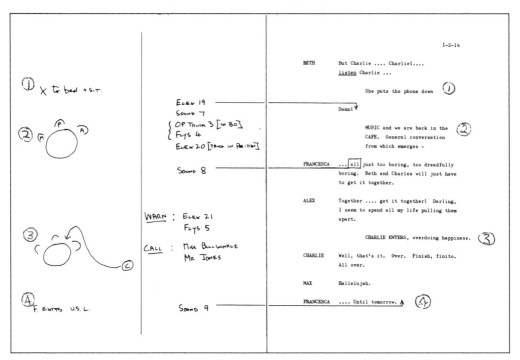

PERFORMANCE

In performance, the DSM stays in the corner, the ASM(s) roam the stage checking and double checking, and the stage manager pops between stage and auditorium. All members of the team are continuously anticipating disaster, have thought about all the possible but improbable things that could go wrong, and have planned how they will extricate the show from such disasters. The senior stage manager will usually be on stage at critical moments like curtain up and curtain calls, but will spend part of each performance watching from the auditorium to ensure that the actors remain faithful to the original production.

Stage management is essentially about controlling people rather than things. Good stage managers have to be so technically competent that they can solve staging problems almost subconsciously. This allows them to give full concentration to the management of people – both acting people and technical people.

5   Scenery

This book is concerned with practicalities rather than aesthetics – with the practical realisation of a scene design rather than the ideas which have determined that design's format and style. This does not mean that scene designers, scene builders and scene shifters should work in non-communicating cells. Scene designers will not get very far if they do not understand something of the way in which scenery is built and moved. And those who build and move scenery will communicate more easily with the designer if they have an interest in, and knowledge of, the design process.

The available stage and its facilities, the available money and time are certainly factors that must be considered in establishing the form of scenery. This is not necessarily a heavy restriction on the designer's creativity. Within the limitations of the quantities, shapes and movements of scenic elements it is still possible to design in a wide range of styles.

HIDDEN SCENIC COSTS

When accusations of scenic extravagance are made, theatres often respond by pointing out that the major part of their budget is devoted to salary costs and that the outlay on scenic materials is a very small portion of total expenditure. However, a small increase in the complexity of scenery can produce a larger increase in running costs due to the extra labour and/or time required to set up the scenery before the performance and move it during the performance. This is particularly true of theatres performing in repertoire with daily changeovers: a significant proportion of the total personnel costs can be attributed to the complexities of the daily changeover – often requiring overtime and overnight working.

Indeed there may be a case for incurring extra production costs to build scenery in a way that will make its handling less labour intensive in performance. *All* the financial implications must be considered seriously in the early stages of a scenic design.

COST EFFECTIVENESS

To help control costs, it is useful to have as detailed a breakdown as possible of individual scenic item costings, particularly if the design has to be trimmed to come within budget. It is surprising just how often the more expensive items of detailing on a set can be the least effective in communicating the production's intentions to the audience. Comparison of cost and effect can be a useful approach to keeping a design within budget.

MASKING

In most productions the technical areas of the stage are hidden from audience view. This masking often has to be added – almost as an afterthought – by the technical staff using neutral borders at the top and neutral legs or wings at the side. Masking, however, should be part of the design: good masking not only conceals the technical area but defines the performance area. Ideally a design will be self-masking. The various elements of the setting will define what the audience should see and conceal what they should not – perhaps with the addition of just a high black border and a couple of discreet black legs for the benefit of those sitting in the difficult masking positions at the ends of the front rows. One popular design format is a permanent decorative surround which masks while giving unity to a series of scenes defined by the minimum of representational objects.

Masking should be worked out in plan and section at the drawing board by checking lines of sight from extreme seating positions. Some production styles deliberately leave technical areas (particularly lighting equipment) unmasked – but the amount of unmasked area should be a calculated decision rather than left to chance.

STANDING OR CHANGEABLE

If the action of a script does not require changes in location, the performance will require only one set. If this set is for a run of performances on only one stage, it may be constructed from relatively heavy materials and fixed together by relatively unsophisticated means. If it is to be toured, however, or played in repertoire, light construction and speedy assembly are advisable in the interests of budgeting and scheduling. In the case of scenery changed during a performance, sophisticated construction becomes essential rather than just advisable. The time and staff available for the scene change will determine the degree of sophistication required.

There has been a move away from completely changeable scenery where 'scene change' implied a complete replacement of everything behind the proscenium. This is not due entirely to economics, although cost considerations do play a significant part in restricting the amount of scenery. It results largely from the aesthetic aim of establishing style by the presence from scene to scene of constant unifying elements.

Consequently much of today's scenery tends to consist of a basic standing set with changeable elements.

SCENERY MOVEMENTS

Scenery changes may be hidden from the audience by a curtain or by a blackout, or they may be incorporated into the action. Scenery moving in view (an old technique enjoying a revival) should be designed and built to move without visible human assistance. Costumed staff or actors can assist a visual change but such a change is usually more effective if the assistance appears to be delicate rather than heavily physical.

VERTICAL OR HORIZONTAL

Scenery can be moved vertically or horizontally. On the huge operatic stages of Central Europe, complete scenes can be lowered into the basement and some smaller simpler stages around the world have various elevators and traps which allow a limited lowering of parts of the scene. In most cases, however, vertical movement of scenery means hoisting upwards into a fly tower above the stage.

Horizontal movement of scenery to storage spaces (scene docks) at the side of the stage can be done manually by planning the set so that it breaks down into pieces which can be carried, preferably by not more than two people. Alternatively, sections of the set can be assembled on wheeled platforms (trucks) for easier movement. On the bigger opera stages there are often huge sliding platform-stages which can move a complete scene from the acting area into an off-stage dock.

HEMP FLYING

The simplest form of flying is hoisting scenery into the fly tower by sheer brute force – manual heaving on ropes without any assistance from machinery, counterweights or pulley systems giving mechanical advantage. This simple form of flying is usually known as *hemp* and a theatre equipped in this way is referred to as a *hemp house* – the word 'hemp' indicating the original type of rope. The work is done from a gallery at the side of the stage known as the *fly floor* from which the ropes pass up to the *grid* (a supporting frame for pulley blocks at the top of the fly tower) and down to the stage. Each set of flying ropes consists of three lines: the *long*, the *centre* and the *short*, named with reference to distance from the fly gallery.

The ropes are tied-off on the fly gallery to large wooden or metal cleats. There are normally two rows of these cleat rails: the bottom row for the lowered position of the scenery and the top row for the raised position. These positions are known as *deads* (*trims* in America). The bottom dead of a cloth, for example, is when the bottom of the cloth is absolutely straight and just, only just, touching the stage floor – that is, touching without the floor taking any of the cloth's weight, for that would result in creases. When deading, instructions are given to the fly crew in terms of in (down) and out (up) on the short, centre and long: for example, 'in on your short, out on your long'. The lines are kept tied off on the bottom dead cleat and when the scenery is flown out of sight it is tied off on the top dead. Any piece of scenery flown as high as possible is said to be *gridded*. Sets of lines not in use are tied to a sandbag to provide weight for lowering to stage level when next required.

Hemp flying

Whereas gauzes, borders and light cloths can be handled in this way, the sheer weight of built scenery makes it difficult to fly smoothly. Moreover hemp flying is not just wasteful of manpower but is rather unpleasant work. Mechanical assistance can be given by rigging a pulley system with mechanical advantage – a billy-block – and this is particularly useful for the heaviest pieces. However, the real solution lies in counterweight flying.

COUNTERWEIGHT FLYING

Here the weight of the flown scenery is counterbalanced by an appropriate number of weights, usually iron but occasionally lead, in a vertically travelling cradle. Steel wires run from this cradle over grid pulleys to a metal bar the width of the stage. As the width of stage increases, more suspension wires are provided and the single bar becomes a pair of bars with cross-bracing. A rope loop running from the top of the cradle up to the grid, down to the stage floor and back to the bottom of the cradle allows one person to fly pieces of any weight in or out, provided that the correct number of counterweights has been added to the cradle. Ideally the cradle has the same travel as the bar and scenery which it is counterbalancing – that is, from grid to stage floor. In this case, the weight in the cradle will equal the weight to be flown. In some situations, particularly when there is restricted wall space due to the stage being wider than the fly tower, or when there is restricted height above scene dock doors, all or some of the cradles can only travel half the distance of their fly bars. In these circumstances a system known as *double purchase* is used, with the cradle carrying twice the weight of the load.

Counterweight flying

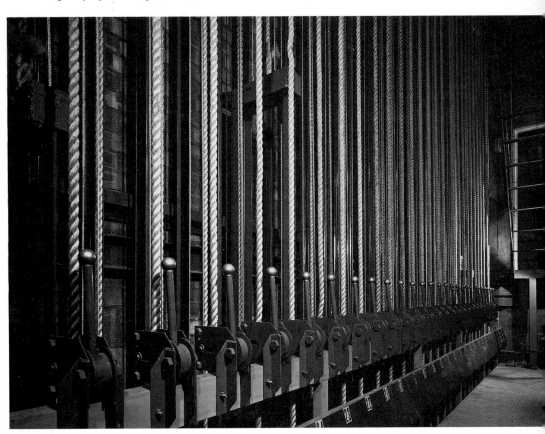

Since the weights must be added to the cradle after the scenery has been attached, the weighting has to be done when the cradle is high (near the grid) corresponding to the bar being low (near the stage). Therefore there has to be a loading gallery just below grid level. While scenery is being hung a member of the fly crew is positioned in this gallery to add weights to the cradles as necessary.

SAFETY IN FLYING

Safety routines are very important in counterweight flying. Weights must not be added to the cradle until the scenery is attached to the bar and, conversely, scenery must not be removed from a bar until the counterweights have been removed. Otherwise the overweighted bar will run dangerously fast to the grid. Counterweight sets have a lock which clamps on the handling rope and this should always be clamped when the set is not being handled. These locks, however, are not intended to hold a bar that is incorrectly weighted.

In hemp flying it is vital that no lines are untied from a cleat unless it is absolutely certain that enough crew are standing by to take the weight.

In all flying, particularly during fit-ups, rehearsals and get-outs, it is essential that the fly crew have a clear view of that part of the stage where the flown scenery will land or take off. Where the crew operating the lines cannot see, they should work under instructions from someone who can see.

Single purchase counterweights can be operated from a fly gallery or from stage level. Double purchase can only operate from a gallery. There are bonus points either way. At stage level the fly crew may see more clearly and be in better contact with other stage staff and stage management. In a fly gallery the atmosphere may be calmer and concentrated on one technical job; also it is easier to have advance warning of scenic pieces in the fly tower fouling one another.

Anything hanging above a stage must be regarded as a potential source of danger only to be averted by constant vigilance over such matters as knots, over-strained wires, etc. – not to mention hammers and other tools hooked 'temporarily' over a bar while working.

ADVANCED FLYING SYSTEMS

Hydraulic and electric power is applied to flying with two objectives: firstly to simplify performances by allowing one person to operate several bars moving at different speeds in different directions and, secondly, to simplify rigging by making the system self-balancing and thus free from the labour of manual counterweighting. The most elaborate of these systems is based on a series of single wire hoists which can be linked in any combination by a computer. However, it is a matter of concern to many experienced theatre technicians that some of

Computer control of
motorised flying
(Bytecraft Pty Ltd)

the advanced flying systems now being installed do not include adequate provision for manual operation if the machinery develops faults.

FLOWN SCENERY   Painted cloths, where the thickish paint would crack and crease if the
cloth were folded, are normally fixed to timber battens at top and
bottom by sandwiching the cloth between two pieces of wood. The
cloth is stored and moved by rolling on its bottom batten. For hemp
flying the ropes are tied directly to the top batten. For counterweight
flying the batten is suspended from the fly bar with chains. Dyed and
thinly painted cloths and gauzes are usually supplied with tapes at the
top and a pocket at the bottom. The tapes can be tied directly on to the
fly bar (or on to a timber batten in a hemp house) and the pocket can
either be filled with chain or, better, a length of screwed electrical
conduit which will keep a gauze straight and stretched. This type of
cloth is folded for storage. For ease in hanging, all cloths and gauzes
should have their centres clearly marked.

(*left*) Drapes or gauzes may be tied directly to the bars of a counterweight system. (*right*) Battened cloths are hung by chains.

A *French flat* is a flown flat or series of flats battened together for flying. The weight must be taken from the bottom of the flat where a steel wire is attached to a hanging iron screwed or bolted to the timber framework. This wire is kept flush to the flat by passing it through a ring screwed to the top of the flat. The amount of wire between the top of the flat and the fly bar is known as the *drift* and care must be taken in calculation and measurement to ensure that it is not too short (the bar would come into sight) or too long (the flat would not fly completely out of sight). The portion of drift wire in sight is often painted black to avoid its glistening in the light. Black plastic-sheathed flying wire is now available for use, subject to particularly careful safety checking for hidden corrosion.

FLY PLOTS

All sets of flying lines are numbered from downstage and are usually at fixed intervals of between 6 in and 9 in (150mm and 300mm). In addition to the fixed numbering it is common practice to chalk the name of the flying piece (e.g. 'ballroom FF' or 'garden BC') on the frame adjacent to the cradle. Deads are marked on the ropes with coloured tape. Fly crew usually keep two plots: a hanging plot listing the items on each bar, and a running plot of the bars that move on each cue.

SPOT LINES

When a single line is required for an effect, a lighting boom or perhaps to pick up something like the curved end of a cyclorama bar, a temporary *spot line* is dropped through the grid at the required position. If this line is to move on cue, it can be fed over pulleys to the fly gallery; if

SHOW: MERRY FLEAPIT

40	CYC
39	BALLROOM B.C.
38	GARDEN GAUZE
37	
36	LX
35	LX
34	
33	
32	PORTAL 3
31	GARDEN CUT
30	BALLROOM CUT
29	
28	LX
27	
26	CONSERVATORY F.F.
25	BALLROOM CUT
24	KITCHEN BACKING
23	BLACK BORDER
22	CONSERVATORY CUT
21	
20	
19	KITCHEN F.F.
18	PORTAL 2
17	GARDEN CUT
16	LIBRARY CLOTH
15	BALLROOM CUT
14	
13	LX
12	BLACK LEGS
11	KITCHEN F.F.
10	BLACKS
9	CONSERVATORY CUT
8	SHOW CLOTH
7	GAUZE
6	
5	LX
4	LX
3	PORTAL 1 (SHOW PILES)
2	HOUSE BORDER
1	HOUSE TABS

The hanging plot (*left*) lists the items suspended from each set of hemp lines or counterweight bar.

The fly plot (*below*) records which items have to be flown in or out on each cue.

FLY PLOT

SHOW: MERRY FLEAPIT   ACT: I

Q	MOVE	PRESET
		8, 17, 31, 38, 40
1	8 OUT	
2	7 + 10 IN	17, 31, 38 OUT
3	10 OUT (BLACKS)	
4	7 OUT (GAUZE)	
5	22 IN	26 IN (WHEN TRUCK SET)
6	8 IN	29 + 26 OUT / 19 + 24 IN
7	8 OUT (FAST)	
8	7 + 10 IN	19 + 24 OUT
9	7 + 10 OUT	
10	7 + 10 IN	16 IN
11	10 OUT	

movement is not required, it is often tied off to fixings immediately above the grid.

THE ROLE OF FLYING

Flying is a very useful method for storing and moving *two-dimensional* scenery. It is the only satisfactory way of handling cloths, and it is a useful way of handling framed scenery provided that it sets parallel to the front of the stage. This is the main limitation of flying – it can only handle scenery in quantity if everything flies in one plane. It is possible to fly on the oblique but one flown flat set on an angle blocks all the lines between the upstage and downstage limits of that flat: the steeper the angle, the more lines blocked.

It is possible to fly flats parallel for storage, then set them on the oblique when they are at stage level, but this requires a tricky operation known as *overhauling*. After the scenery reaches the stage, the bar is lowered further until there is enough slack on the drift wires to allow the flat to be angled. To do this the fly crew have to pull against the counterweights as they are no longer in counterbalance with the scenery. The technique has to be used with caution and is only advisable when the scenery is relatively lightweight and the scene change is not visible to the audience.

For changes carried out in sight of the audience, flying can be quick and graceful. For horizontal movements, curtains and gauzes may be hung from *tab tracks*: either the standard overlapping twin track with a pair of tabs opening from the centre outwards, or a single *wipe* track where a single curtain can be drawn over all or part of the stage. Conventional tracks bunch from the onstage end of the track. *Rear-fold* tracks bunch at the off-stage and this can be a rather more elegant movement.

Generally speaking, counterweight flying is a very cost-effective way of handling scenery: once a piece is tied on to a bar and counter-weighted, it can be handled with ease, accuracy and certainty by one person.

SUSPENSION ON SMALL STAGES

There are many proscenium stages without fly towers. Unfortunately many of these stages also have limited wing space or even none at all. But if there is no flying space, there is often hanging space: material can be suspended but not flown out. At worst there may be only a couple of feet and its use restricted to lighting equipment and masking borders. Cloths can be flown out of sight by *rolling*. The cloth is slowly lowered while a team rolls it on to the bottom batten after which it can be flown out of sight. For rolling in sight of an audience it is possible to arrange lines to roll the cloth from the bottom on a special large diameter round timber.

With slightly more hanging space available, it is possible to fly a cloth in half its height by *tumbling*. The cloth is raised on two sets of lines, one set from the top and one from the bottom. To smooth the operation, an unattached round timber may be rolled in the fold. Alternatively, the second set of lines may be attached to a timber batten attached midway up the cloth and the two halves flown simultaneously.

The main hope for such a stage is to ensure that as many lines as possible are available. Minimum line and pulley provision is often made on the assumption that masking will be hung on *dead lines* tied from the top of a ladder. This is frustrating and time wasting.

The only true solution to a poorly equipped or non-orthodox stage is to accept its limitations and adopt a scenic style that tries to make imaginative use of what exists, rather than try to force the technical facilities to do something for which they were never intended.

BUILT SCENERY

The aim of good scenery construction is a three-dimensional structure which can be assembled very quickly from two-dimensional components. If these component pieces are absolutely flat, they can be packed in a very tight wing space ready for assembly in a quick scene change. They will also take up minimum space in stores and transport trucks. The traditional *flat* is canvas stretched over a timber frame with every detail, including three-dimensional mouldings, expressed in paint. With the growth of naturalistic styles of production, real mouldings have become an increasing feature of flat construction. Where these mouldings are relatively thin they can be fixed permanently, but pieces of any considerable thicknesss should be provided with bolts to allow removal for transportation. The search for realism has led to flats being faced with plywood rather than canvas. While such flats may be fine for a permanent set, their weight complicates scene changing by requiring more staff and more time.

Flats supported by brace and weight (*left*). French braces (*right*) hinged so that they may be folded against the flat for packing or flying.

The traditional method of joining flats is by line and cleat: the join is quick to make and, just as important, quick to break. Heavier timber flats, or canvas flats top-heavy with cornices, etc., are often pin-hinged together. This method is firm and positive but it is in no way quick.

Joining flats by line
and cleat.

Placing the top on a
folding rostrum.

A well-designed and well-constructed set should almost stand up by
mutual support, especially on a stage without a rake. Normally the flats
will join at an angle and in an endeavour to give an impression of
solidity there are likely to be quite a few pillars made from narrow flats
(jogs) meeting at right angles. Where necessary, support is given by

braces, either the standard adjustable-length brace hooked into a screw eye on the flat and weighted or screwed on to the floor, or a *French brace* hinged to the flat and weighted to the stage.

Contemporary scene design makes very little use of the technique of scene changing by building complete sets from flats. Standing box-sets of realistic rooms are still built from flattage but, if a scene change is required, a more representational scenic style is likely to be adopted. The ever increasing weight of materials used in scene design and the need to reduce labour costs, together with the desire to let scenes flow continuously into one another rather than be broken by waits, has encouraged techniques of flying and trucking rather than manhandling. As a result, recent years have seen an increase in the amount of heavy handling involved in the setting-up preparations for a performance but a reduction in such handling during the performance.

TRUCKING

A lot of scenery is mounted on castored platforms called trucks. Although a small scene may be mounted on a single truck, it is common to use several trucks, rather in the nature of sub-assemblies. These are small enough to be stored in restricted wing space yet relatively quick to push into position on the stage. The individual scenic elements usually pin-hinge to each other and to the truck base: the result is quite solid and rigid. Wherever possible the individual bits are flat for transportation.

A small scene set on a truck to simplify setting and striking.

FALSE STAGES   When trucks are required to move 'magically' in sight of the audience without too obvious a visible means of propulsion, it is possible to tack temporary slender timber guiding strips to the stage floor and man-oeuvre the trucks with crew concealed behind them or with lines or rods manipulated from the wings. But floor guides make life difficult for actors and impossible for dancers. So, a false stage floor is laid for complex productions, particularly big musicals. This has tracks cut into it to guide the trucks, which are pulled to and fro by steel wire cables laid in the cavity between the stage and the false floor. Movement is by hand winches or motors.

REVOLVES   Revolving turntables may be built into the stage floor as part of the permanent equipment, or laid on top of the stage as part of the production. The temporary revolve is the most adaptable as it can be made the appropriate size for each production. Drive is often by hand winch for temporary revolves, although usually by motor for permanent equipment. Revolves can be used to shift scenery with the curtain down or in a blackout, but they are more interesting when used as a means of keeping the production flowing from scene to scene while the actors continue the action. Apart from the conventional single revolve, twin revolves side by side have been used to good effect, particularly in musicals – each revolve changing the scenery on its own half of the stage.

Revolving stage designed for quick assembly (Ziller Technik).

A Central European
stage (Warsaw Opera)
with machinery in the
German cruciform
tradition (see sketch).
Note also another
smaller theatre in the
same building
complex.

MAIN
STAGE

PROSCENIUM

MECHANISED STAGES

In some parts of the world, mainly in Central European countries with a long tradition of repertoire opera, stages have extensive machinery installations. The main stage area is broken up into a series of elevator sections which can sink below the stage or rise above it. In some cases the understage area is so deep that entire scenes can be set below and brought up to stage level. There are various formats of wagon stage, but perhaps the most frequently used is the cruciform. This uses three wagons (left, right and centre) which are the same size as the main stage acting area. These wagons, carrying complete scenes, can be driven on to the main stage as required. In the off-stage position, large sound-proof shutters allow scenes to be changed on the wagons while the performance continues. There are many variations of the engineered stage including enormous revolves of a diameter much wider than the proscenium opening and with huge scenic lifts built in.

STUDIO STAGES

At the other end of the scale are performances staged with planks and passion. Some studio stages are quite elaborately adaptable while others are just a bare room enclosing actor and audience. There is only one desirable common structural factor for all studios: bars of standard scaffolding diameter at strategic points on ceiling and walls to provide a universal fixing. Ideally this should form an all-over grid with the bars spaced to provide a symmetrically sized module.

MATERIALS

There seems to be no limitation on the type of materials used in today's stage decor. This is partly a result of the search for new textures and partly because representational styles of design require the representative objects to have what can only be called 'truth', resulting in a move away from fake and illusion towards real materials.

In practical terms this means that scenery has become heavier. The tendency of flats to be covered in plywood rather than canvas has already been mentioned. Large chunks of metal, sometimes tortured to produce a textured sculptural surface, have become popular, as have structures built of expanded-metal shapes. GRP (glass reinforced plastic, often called 'fibreglass') and similar modern synthetics can be less weight to handle but roughened textures, which respond sympathetically to light, can be brutal to hands. Foam plastics are very easy to work: indeed they are so easy that they need a gauze appliqué to stop them crumbling at the edges.

Decisions about materials for cloths, gauzes and borders are closely linked with lighting.

Cloths flown on rollers above a stage with restricted height.

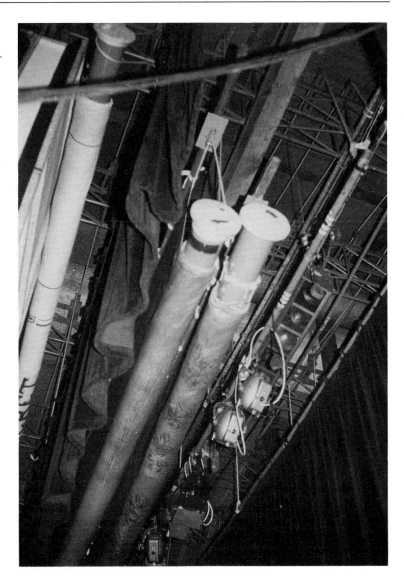

FIREPROOFING A major restriction on choice of material is fire risk. Actual regulations vary from country to country and in Britain the finer points are subject to the interpretation of the fire prevention officer within whose jurisdiction a particular theatre is situated. In judging borderline cases the fire officer usually takes into account a personal assessment of the local stage staff, particularly the resident stage manager. This makes a lot of sense since fire prevention owes a great deal to the sort of careful responsible attitiudes that go beyond the chapter and verse of regulations.

Restrictions on materials are naturally more stringent in open stage theatres or on apron stages thrusting beyond the fire curtain. In conventional theatres, the proscenium wall is a fire-wall in which every opening has a fire-resistant door so that, once the fire curtain has been lowered, a combination of fire-wall, smoke lantern and sprinklers will retard the spread of the fire until the auditorium has been evacuated.

Fire resistance is either an intrinsic property of a material or is super-imposed by surface application of chemicals. Whenever possible, theatres buy ready fireproofed materials for scenic construction. Non-fireproof materials can be treated with fireproofing solutions or fire-retarding paints. The fireproofing of fabrics, particularly gauzes, tends to wear off with time. Long-running fabrics should be checked from time to time with a match (if you don't do it, the fire officer certainly will) and resprayed if necessary.

PAINTING

From the early 1960s to the early 1980s, the art and craft of pictorial scene painting began to decline due to lack of demand. The pictorial style grew so unfashionable that it became quite difficult to find painters with the training and experience to realise designs incorporating 'traditional' perspective cloths, gauzes and borders. The trend was reversed just in time, but the role of paint in many of today's design styles remains textural. Developments in synthetic paints have simplified some of the problems of dealing with newer materials.

PROJECTED SCENERY

Projection should not be regarded as a cheap and easy alternative to painted scenery. Full-scale projection is complex and expensive: it is a technique to be used when the visual style of the production requires frequent and rapid changes of location and an atmosphere of translucent images. Most European operatic stages have full projection equipment as part of their permanent installation, with the projectors located on properly positioned galleries. With few exceptions, projection in the rest of the world requires a temporary installation of expensive equipment and there are frequently problems arising from lack of depth on a shallow stage. Anyone tempted by projection should budget early and schedule additional time for pre-planning and for technical rehearsals. On the small stage, images from 35mm slide projectors of the carousel type can be an interesting component of non-realistic design.

MODELS

The basis of any scenic design is the model and the ground plan, both normally on the scale of half inch to the foot (metricated at 1:25). At least one section (on the centre line) is required in order to work out hanging and masking with accuracy. Two-dimensional sketches, particularly in the form of storyboards, are useful accessories to indicate the atmosphere of particular scenes but they are no substitute for models, plans and sections.

Most scenery is designed in model form.

COMPUTER AIDED DESIGN

While full CAD (Computer Aided Design) is still relatively rare in the theatre world, experimental work in progress suggests that it will become an increasingly important support tool. While the scale model seems likely to remain the core scene-design artefact – both as working method and as statement of intention – the potential of computers as design aids makes their growing use inevitable. Areas where they can offer particular support to the designer, both when working alone and when in discussion with the director and other members of the design team, include access to image banks, manipulation of images, rapid scaling experiments and instant viewing from alternative sightlines. There is already a fast accelerating use of computer drafting systems to produce stage scenery plans and adapt them for touring (as discussed in chapter 15).

BAUPROBE

The 'Bauprobe' or 'build rehearsal' is a Central European institution that could perhaps have wider application in more theatres producing their own shows. Once a design is close to being finalised, it is set up roughly on stage using substitute flats, rostra, cloths, furniture, etc. Two things come out of this. Firstly the director, designer and choreographer are able to move about the dimensioned mock-up set to find out if the spacing is as they require. Secondly, minor adjustments in dimensions to enable the use of items like stock rostra or elevators may be suggested and demonstrated. Such changes may not affect the design concept but may save a lot of money in both initial production costs and daily running costs. However, it is usually easier for the technical staff to 'sell' this sort of idea to directors and designers by practical demonstration rather than by paper discussion.

SCENERY ORGANISATION

The organisation of a production's scenic environment, from fit-up through rehearsals and performance to get-out, is discussed in later chapters on different types of show. Meanwhile the usefulness of a trial set-up in the workshop should be mentioned. Space problems often make this impossible but if the set – or sections of it – can be assembled prior to the stage fit-up, a check can be made on details such as positioning of cleats and hinges. And the director may be able to anticipate problems over matters such as door and step sizes. It is surprising how frequently, despite detailed planning, one hears phrases like 'Oh, I didn't know the door was going to hinge downstage'.

6   Props

The term *properties*, invariably shortened to *props*, covers three over-lapping categories: *furnishings* (from sofas to thrones, and altars to kitchen sinks), *dressings* (from portraits to rubber plants, and tapestries to plaster alsatians) and *hand props* (from swords to martinis and scrolls to telegrams). In all categories there are two kinds of props: *practical props* and the rest. All props look like the real article but practical props also behave like real. However, they are not necessarily real. For example, food that does not have to be eaten could be made from plastic, plaster or papier mâché. Practical grapes for eating would probably have to be the real thing but the practical 'oyster' in an oyster shell could be but half a teaspoonful of clear jelly.

DESIGNING

The visual correctness of all props, whether specially made or not, is the scene designer's responsibility. Before rehearsals commence there will be a detailed prop list, but it is in the very nature of the rehearsal process that prop requirements, especially hand props, will change as the rehearsals proceed. So the stage management must maintain day-to-day liaison with the designer about items added, cut and amended.

Props can be made, bought, hired or borrowed. Some props are so specialised that they can only be made. Others may be available off the shelf, either in ordinary shops or from specialist dealers. Whether such items are made, bought or hired is a budgeting decision which takes into account not just relative initial cost but length of run, time and resources available for making, etc.

MAKING

The designs for large props to be made in the workshop should be in model form but sketches, supplemented by discussion, may be sufficient for smaller items. If a prop is practical, additional discussion is often required between propmaker and stage manager, possibly also director. In the case of comedian's props, direct discussion between propmaker and actor is essential. Many comic's laughs come from the

HADRIAN VII
Processional Cross.

pictures of Saints

central crystal –
small cut glass
salt cellar or large
decanter stopper
possibly a glass door knob

rays – possibly a
plastic chandelier
mounted flat on
ring

pictures of Saints

studs

Twist of
gold.

Cross 2'9" from top to
    pole junction. Arm 1'8"
Pole 3'9" – dark wood
Overall hight 6'6"
Cross bright gold with
    textured ends to arms.

Note – Auditorium procession
    so back of cross will be
    seen.

heavy gold
or red fringe

bright enamel like
colours – varnish

dark wood

Anna Welbourne.

Large props under
construction in the
workshop at West
Yorkshire Playhouse.

manipulation of props and the simplest detail on the simplest prop can
be quite crucial to success.

BUYING AND HIRING

Buying and hiring of props are often delegated to junior members of the
stage management. The designer will always choose furniture and
wherever possible other major items should also be a direct designer
choice. Any other members of the production team selecting items
should reach an understanding with the shop that the item will be
taken back against a refund if returned unharmed in, say, 48 hours. Prop
buyers should bear in mind an old rule of thumb: weekly hire charge
multiplied by length of run should not exceed cost of buying minus a
pessimistic estimate of resale value. This is fine for fixed runs but a bit
tricky for speculative productions in the West End or on Broadway! In
deciding whether to buy or hire, remember also that bought items may
be modified and broken down with paint sprays whereas hired items
must be returned 'as was'. Some items may only be available for hire: if it
is a long run and there is no time to make, it may be worthwhile opening
with a hired prop and making a copy later. The hire contract for props
should include an agreed valuation for insurance.

BORROWING

Borrowing (i.e. hiring without payment) is only possible for very short runs. As the lender is doing a favour, a certain amount of tact is advisable on the part of the borrower. Lenders have been known to regard the action of borrowing an item but failing to use it as an affront to the lender's personal taste! So, sound a bit vague when borrowing – mutter something about 'production not finalised', etc. Don't forget to include the borrowed item on the insurance.

DISCOUNTS, CREDITS AND COMPS

Some props, especially proprietary items, may be obtained at a discount or even free if a programme credit is offered. If this is agreed, it is important to be absolutely meticulous about the insertion of credits and their wording. Always send a copy of the programme to your contact in the firm giving discount. Complimentary tickets can be used to lubricate the prop department's relations with supplying firms: especially with members of firms who go out of their way to be helpful beyond the limits of strictly commercial duty.

RETURNS

A returns list of all hired and borrowed items should be filed with delivery notes and correspondence, this list to include not just ad-dresses but the name of the 'contact' person in each firm. After the opening performance there are usually some discarded items to return and, of course, after the final performance all items should be returned immediately.

REHEARSAL PROPS

Props are required very early in rehearsals – often before they are ready. Substitute *rehearsal props* are therefore provided and they should be as near to the actual props as possible. In cases where there is doubt about the size or shape of a prop, a rehearsal prop or series of alternatives is a useful way of finding out the actual requirement by a process of trial and error. Rehearsal props should be gradually replaced by the real props as they become available so that, by the final run-throughs in the rehearsal room, the actors are using the same hand props as in performance. This removes another variable from the technical and dress rehearsals, allowing concentration on problems which cannot be resolved in the rehearsal room.

ORGANISING THE PROPS

Because there is usually such a large number of assorted items, props probably call for more detailed organisation (checking, double-checking and re-checking) than any other staging department. The basis of this organisation is plots, with prop plots falling into two categories: check plots and running plots.

CHECK PLOTS

A check plot for any given point during the show will list the position of every single prop whether set on stage, standing by in the wings, or in the possession of an actor. Where props must be set in a special way, the check plot will include a drawing to show these positions. There will always be a check plot for the prop situation at the beginning of the show, and if there is any considerable movement of props, then there will be further check plots for key points in the progress of the action, particularly interval breaks.

Prop check plot (*left*)
and prop running plot
(*right*)

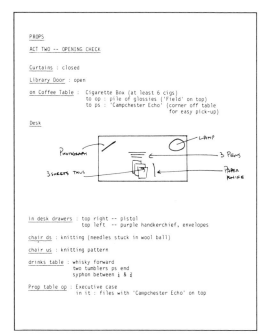

PROPS

ACT TWO -- OPENING CHECK

Curtains : closed

Library Door : open

on Coffee Table : Cigarette Box (at least 6 cigs)
                   to op : pile of glossies ('Field' on top)
                   to ps : 'Campchester Echo' (corner off table
                                               for easy pick-up)

Desk

PHOTOGRAPH   LAMP
                                                    3 PENS
3 SHEETS THUS   PAPER
                                                    KNIFE

in desk drawers : top right -- pistol
                  top left -- purple handkerchief, envelopes

chair ds : knitting (needles stuck in wool ball)

chair us : knitting pattern

drinks table : whisky forward
               two tumblers ps end
               syphon between 1 & 2

Prop table op : Executive case
                in it : files with 'Campchester Echo' on top

O.P. PROPS

When cloth IN

  2 men - STRIKE kitchen table
            Mop-up slosh
            SET throne
  1 man - Hand tray to waiter as he enters in F.C.
            Collect glasses from chorus on exit

When throne room scene started

            STAND BY to give glasses to chorus
            as they enter U.S.
            Position witch's chariot ready for
            donkey (dancers in skin)
            Collect glasses as chorus exit screaming
            Give shoes and hammers to children
            for fairy cobblers' scene

When gauze IN

            STRIKE throne
            SET mushrooms for first half finale
     then - STAND-BY to collect props from fairy
            cobblers on exit below false pros

RUNNING PLOTS

Running plots show the prop cues. Some of these cues are props to be *set* (placed in position on the stage) or *struck* (removed from the stage) during a scene change. Other prop cues involve handing props to actors before making an entrance and collecting props from actors after making an exit. In a scene change with a lot of striking and setting, the plot will list the actions of each individual member of the prop staff. The actions must be integrated so that props are changed in the correct sequence. Quite frequently the changing of the scenery cannot commence until certain props, often fragile, have been struck. Sometimes all the furniture can be moved quickly downstage to clear the scene and then taken off. Whenever possible, prop staff avoid double journeys by trying to set and strike at the same time.

PROP ROOMS Many theatres have a prop room opening directly on to the stage. In addition to providing storage for smaller props, such a room usually has a bench and tools for minor repairs, and facilities (water, sink, cooker, etc.) for preparing prop meals and washing crockery. In theatres with limited facilities the prop room tends to double, unofficially, as a staff green room: this custom, pleasant though it is, should be resisted.

PROP TROLLEYS In some repertoire theatres, particularly in Central Europe, the props for each production are kept on wheeled storage trolleys so that the appropriate show can be brought quickly to the stage each day.

PROP TABLES When there are lots of hand props, it is useful to lay them out on prop tables in the wings if space is available. The 'propiest' shows are often naturalistic box set plays in which there can be so many actor entrances with props that there has to be a prop table outside every door. For long runs, check plots can be pinned to the table and the table may be marked off with labelled sections for each prop to aid an at-a-glance check.

PERSONAL PROPS The personal props that actors carry in their pockets need particular care since they are often handed to other actors or left on the set during the action. Most actors like to keep personal props in their dressing rooms and part of the pre-performance check is to make sure that all the necessary bits and pieces are definitely in the dressing rooms. Prop staff need to enlist the aid of the actors' dressers in returning props to the correct dressing rooms.

REPLACEMENT PROPS If props have to be replaced due to breakages or wearing out during the run, tell the actors and show them the new prop if it is in any way different. Actors in a long run have been known to dry completely on their first entrance when faced with the sight of a new carpet.

7 Lighting

Lighting is perhaps the most fundamental of all the staging techniques: there is not much point in the actors doing their stuff if the audience cannot see them. Moreover, by varying the colour, direction and balance of the light the attention of the audience can be focused on the appropriate part of the stage, and the actor can be clothed in an environment where the atmosphere is fluid but under precise control. For some considerable time lighting was the growth area in theatre technology and, although sound now leads the development field, an apparent air of glamour still surrounds the mysteries of the art and craft of stage lighting.

It is with the craft rather than the art that we are concerned here: the realisation of the design rather than the design itself. Art and craft are not, of course, separate little boxes. The art puts continual pressure on the craft to find ways and means of turning new ideas into reality, and the art is constantly stimulated by the craft possibilities of new technology.

But the hard truth is that there is no point in having the most marvellous idea if that idea cannot be realised because there is neither the technology nor the time available. *Time* is the biggest problem in lighting management. No matter how well the lighting has been pictured in imagination and planned on paper, it takes a long time to rig spotlights, focus them on the desired parts of the stage, and balance the appropriate combination for each cue in the lighting plot. Although rigging can be carried out while the scenery is being assembled, focusing and plotting can only be done satisfactorily once the scenic fit-up is complete. Being the last item in the staging schedule prior to the technical rehearsal with actors, the lighting rehearsal is under pressure to make up any time lost prior to this point. Consequently, to make the greatest possible creative use of this critical phase of the staging, particularly detailed advanced planning is an absolute must.

LIGHTING DESIGNER

The person responsible for planning the lighting is the lighting de- signer. This job can be doubled with director, designer, stage manager or chief electrician, but in most productions there is quite enough work involved to keep one person fully employed on lighting design alone. If the job is doubled, the person taking on the additional responsibiity for lighting design must understand the full extent of pre-planning required.

The lighting designer has to be not only a mixture of artist and technician but a good chairman as well. Lighting is not superimposed but distilled from the ideas of author, composer, director, designer and choreographer as well as lighting designer. There is often a considerable degree of compromise involved and it is the lighting designer who must resolve any conflicts of opinion among the production team, and evolve an acceptable unified concept that is capable of execution with the resources available.

LIGHTING EQUIPMENT

Before considering lighting procedures, we should take a brief look at the tools of the lighting trade – the lights and the control systems.

Floods

All stage lights (once called 'lanterns' but now more commonly 'instruments' or just 'lights') consist of a lamp and optical system contained in a box with pivoting devices to allow pointing in any direction by means of a combination of two movements: up and down in a vertical axis (*tilting*) and side to side in a horizontal axis (*panning*). Where the light leaves the box, there are grooves to take a framed colour filter. The simplest form is the *flood* where the optical system is a fixed reflector. There are no adjustments other than tilt and pan, so there is no possibility of adjusting the size of area lit other than by altering the distance between the flood and the area that it is pointing at. Floods are only useful for lighting large scenic areas such as cycloramas and cloths. The lack of control over beam size and shape makes the flood unsuitable for lighting actors.

(*left*) 500w asymmetric linear flood (Teatro); (*right*) 500w floods linked together for colour mixing (Teatro)

Focus spots   The simplest form of spotlight has a lamp and reflector which together move backwards and forwards in relation to a fixed plano-convex lens. This movement gives control of the beam *size*. An optional four-door rotatable barndoor shutter attached to the front of a focus spotlight allows the beam to be roughly shaped.

Fresnel spots   On a fresnel spotlight, the lamp and reflector move in relation to a fixed fresnel lens which has a stepped front and mottled back giving a characteristic soft-edged quality to the light. A by-product of the soft-edged lens is a certain amount of stray light scattered outside the main beam and this can be distracting on scenery (especially masking borders or wings) adjacent to the spotlight. The scatter can be reduced and some control of beam shape gained by fitting a barndoor to the front of the instrument.

(*left*) Pc focus spot (Selecon)

(*right*) Fresnel spot, showing access for lamp changing. (Teatro)

Profile spots

The profile spotlight gives accurate control of beam *size, shape* and *quality*. The lamp and reflector are stationary: movement of the lens adjusts the quality of the beam edge to the required degree of hardness or softness. Size and shape of the beam are controlled at the optical centre of the system where a set of four shutters provides any desired size of four-sided shapes with straight edges. Adjacent to these shutters is a slot (known as the 'gate') where an adjustable iris diaphragm may be inserted to produce circular beams of the required size. Alternatively a purpose-made mask (known as a *gobo*) may be used for specialised shaping. This type of spotlight is called 'profile' because it projects a profiled image of whatever shape is placed at the gate. The reflector is often ellipsoidal and so profile spots are sometimes known as *ellipsoidals*, especially in America.

Variable beam profile spots

In most profile spotlights, beam size and edge quality are controlled by differential movement of a pair of lenses. The shutters are then used only for shaping. Zooming a pair of lenses makes a wider range of beam angles available from a single spotlight and this makes them particularly suitable for repertoire and multi-use stages.

(*right*) Leko profile spot (Strand Lighting)

(*left*) Cantata 18/32 variable beam profile spot (Strand Lighting)

Beamlights

All the lens spotlights described above produce a conical beam and therefore the spread of light increases with the throw distance. The beamlight family have no lenses but the parabolic shape of their special reflector produces a parallel beam which lights the same size of area whatever the throw.

PAR lamps have, built into the lamp's design, a disposable optical system giving a near-parallel beam. Used in a simple can with only pan and tilt adjustments, these PAR lamps make useful members of the beamlight family, particularly when several are used together for a broad effect.

Follow spots

The spotlights which operators use to follow actors around the stage are normally high-powered profile spots with sophisticated pan and tilt mountings for smooth movement. The high light output is derived from discharge lamps (known as CSI or HMI) which can only be dimmed satisfactorily by means of a mechanical shutter. Low voltage beamlights are also used, particularly in European opera houses and mega musicals. Their soft-edged parallel beam accommodates the human figure neatly from knees/waist to head on all throws without any need to adjust beam size.

Parcan (Strand Lighting)

Follow spot (Selecon)

Scene projectors   Discharge lamps have opened up new horizons in scene projection
where conventional 5kW and even 10kW tungsten lamps do not give
enough brightness. All projectors require complex condenser-lens systems, high quality objective lenses and forced cooling. Good equipment
is therefore very expensive. Projectors for moving-effects discs can use
lower quality optics and require less power. Much projection work,
especially in smaller theatres, uses standard 35mm magazine slide
projectors of the carousel type. Carousels are also used on big productions with a matrix of eighteen or more individual projectors controlled
through a computer.

Scene projector (Pani)

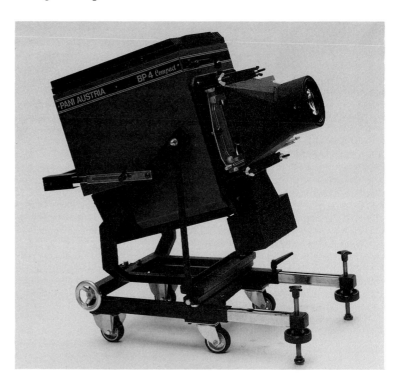

Tungsten halogen   Today's stage lights use tungsten halogen lamps which have a longer life
and are a little brighter than the old tungsten lamps. But probably their
most important feature is that they maintain full brightness throughout
life: there is no gradual loss of light due to blackening of the glass.

Control systems   The central control point for stage lighting is usually referred to as the
board. This is a contraction of 'switchboard' and 'dimmerboard', dating
from the time when stage lighting was operated from a massively
engineered frame of switches and dimmer handles on a platform in the
wings above the prompt corner. These handles moved the sliders of

directly operated mechanical dimmers, which were normally resistances although transformers were sometimes used in the more expensive models. After several interim experiments in miniaturising the boards so that they could be positioned to give the operator a view of the stage, the 1960s brought an electronic revolution to dimmers. This was followed in the 1970s by application of the information technology revolution to the control desks.

All modern systems are two-part: the dimmers and the desk, linked by a slender data line. The dimmer room is the distribution point for electricity to the various sockets positioned around the theatre for feeding lights. The modern dimmer is almost universally a device called a *thyristor*. Most thyristor dimmers are designed to cope with any load between 40w and 2.4kW although larger installations include a handful capable of dealing with up to 6kW. The dimmer room is situated in any convenient backstage position and the desk in an auditorium control room with a clear view of the stage. This is not just an ideal: it is standard practice in all new theatres and in older theatres as they are refurbished. With very few exceptions, all desks are now computer based and are able to record a virtually infinite number of lighting cues for instant playback.

Lighting control at Edinburgh King's Theatre (Strand Lighting Galaxy Nova)

**LIGHTING
PROCEDURE**

Although the lights and the control desk are the obvious tools of lighting design, there is another piece of equipment which is just as important: the *drawing board*. After script study and discussions to formulate a mutually agreed answer to the question 'What is light going to do for us in this production?', the lighting designer must decide:

- Where to put the lights.
- Which lights to put.
- Where to point these lights.
- Which colours in which lights.

These decisions are made at the drawing board. How they are made is not the subject of this book. Our concern is with organisation: what decisions are required, how they are communicated to the other staging departments, how they are integrated with the decisions of these departments, and how they are implemented during the staging period in the theatre. With these procedures in mind, let us follow through the planning and implementation of the lighting design.

PLANS

The basic document is the lighting layout plan. It has two functions: the action of drawing is the means of working towards the decisions, and copies of the completed drawing are the means of communicating these decisions. The basis of the lighting plan is the scene designer's ground plan, normally drawn to a scale of 1:25. The lighting designer works by pinning a sheet of tracing paper to this ground plan and drawing the required equipment in position, using symbols to indicate the various types of lighting instrument. The easiest symbols to use (and subsequently the easier to read) are scale stencils of manufacturer's spotlight shapes.

At the drawing board, the eraser is as important as the pencil. The first attempt nearly always uses too much equipment: too many lights for the money budgeted, too many for the time scheduled, possibly too many for the available electricity and very probably too many for the lighting to have a clean positive quality. A substantial part of the design process is refining down – examining the role of every light to see if it really is essential, often by asking the question, 'What would happen if we did not have this light?' This elimination process usually results in a more practical rig and a cleaner visual effect.

The completed plan shows the types of light, their positions, their colours, and their control channel numbers. Many designers put the colour filter numbers inside the instrument symbols, with the control channel numbers alongside. Notes are made beside the symbols of any special accessories such as gobo, iris, barndoor, etc. After drawing all the lighting equipment, enough detail of the scenery ground plan is traced through to indicate the geographical relationship between lights and scenery.

The aim of an ideal plan is that it should include enough information for the rigging electricians, without the lighting designer being present, to get every light hung in the correct position, with the correct colour and accessories, and fed from the correct dimmer. The lighting designer should be able to walk in at the conclusion of rigging, find no surprises, and start focusing immediately. In practice, a wise lighting designer will try to visit or telephone during the rigging: no matter how immaculate the plans, unforeseen circumstances (often in the shape of revised scenery hangings) may produce a rigging problem requiring lighting revisions.

To communicate their intentions to the rest of the production team, lighting designers should circulate copies of their plans to designer, production manager, production carpenter and stage management, in addition to the electrics crew. To keep the plan as simple to read as possible, detailed focus information is not normally included on these copies of the plan. It is pencilled on the lighting designer's copy and amended while watching run-throughs in the rehearsal room. Indeed one of the problems of lighting plans is that they often have to be drawn – so that equipment can be ordered and such things as colours and cables prepared – before the production takes final shape in rehearsal. This is just something that has to be lived with, remembering that it is easier to alter a plan than to have no plan at all.

SECTIONS

During design work at the drawing board, the lighting designer requires a sectional drawing. For a proscenium show where the flying runs parallel to the setting line, one section through the centre line is usually enough. But for an asymmetric open stage setting, sections taken on several axes may be necessary. On the sectional drawings, the lighting designer can see the angles at which the lights will hit the actors, check the height required for the lighting bars to mask, and if the top and bottom deads of the hanging scenery are shown, check whether the light beams will hit the required scenic pieces when they are flown in, without being obstructed by scenery which is flown out. Software programs are now available which allow lighting designers to work on a computer screen rather than a drawing board. With these programs, the designer can move from plan to section at the stroke of a key, getting an instant visual display of alternative light positions and beam angles.

The finalised drawings, whether from a drawing board or from a computer printer, should include a section showing all the lighting bars at their correct heights (i.e. their *deads*, or, to use the American term which is becoming universal, *trim*). Amazingly, some productions are

A lighting design
section showing the
deads (trims) of the
lighting bars (pipes).

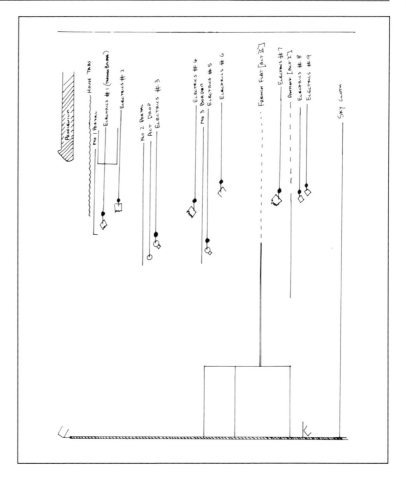

still rigged without the help of a section on which all the deads, both
scenic and lighting, have been decided. This saving of planning time
leads inevitably to a waste of the infinitely more precious staging time.

**EQUIPMENT
SCHEDULES**

From the lighting plan, detailed schedules of lighting requirements are
prepared. These show the numbers of each type of instrument required,
plus listings of accessories and colour filters, and a dimensioned
breakdown of rigging into bars, booms, clamps, brackets and cable.
Computer systems produce all these listing on request, with no more
effort than a keystroke.

HIRE

If additional equipment is required to augment the theatre's stock, a list
of hire requirements can be extracted from the equipment schedule.
Lighting hire has become rather competitive and it is wise to seek

quotations from at least a couple of rental companies. In comparing quotes, relative reputations for service should be taken into account: the cheap-to-rent light requiring cleaning, maintenance and adjustments during rigging and focusing could turn out to be a rather expensive saving.

CUE SYNOPSIS

The lighting designer pops into the rehearsal room from time to time to see how the production is taking shape. From these visits, particularly to run-throughs towards the end of the rehearsal period, and from various discussions with director, set designer, costume designer and choreographer, the lighting designer begins to formulate a clearer and clearer picture of how it will all look. Immediately before moving from rehearsal room to stage, the lighting must be broken down into specific

A lighting cue
synopsis

'Very Good Eddie'   Piccadilly Theatre

LX Cue Synopsis : Act One

Cue	Time	Page	Purpose
Q.1	3 sec	1	House tabs out --- X-fade to act drop light
Q.2	3 sec	1	Act drop out--- bright day
Q.3	10 sec	2	End of opening number --- check upper level
Q.4	8 sec	5	Preparing for number --- small check
Q.5	8 sec	5	Into 'Some Sort of Somebody' --- check
Q.6	8 sec	5	End of number --- restore to Q.2. state
Q.7	6 sec	8	'Size 13 Collar' --- biggish check
Q.8	8 sec	10	Restore (not upper level)
Q.9	6 sec	11	'Bungalow' --- warm
Q.10	5 sec	12	Restore (with upper level)
Q.11	8 sec	14	'Happily Married' --- small build
Q.12	8 sec	17	'Goodnight Boat' --- biggish check
Q.13	8 sec	18	During number --- more check
Q.14	8 sec	18	Restore to Q.8 with mods
Q.15	5 sec	20	'Blues' --- check, cool
Q.16	6 sec	21	Restore
Q.17	6 sec	23	'Hot Dogs' --- build warms & check cools
Q.18	15 sec	26	Restore to Q.16 state
Q.19	6 sec	27	'Million in the Bank' --- re-balance to DS
Q.20	5 sec	27	Restore
Q.21	8 sec	30	'Friend of Mine' --- check
Q.22	8 sec	30	Build for dance --- especially booms
Q.23	8 sec	31	Build--- to about 75%
Q.24	8 sec	31	Restore to Q.20 state
Q.25	5 sec	32	Concentrate centre
Q.26	5 sec	32	Restore to Q.26 plus
Q.27	5 sec	33	House tabs in

cued changes. This list of lighting changes, the *cue synopsis*, gives the Q number, timing, position in script, and a short verbal description of each lighting change. Ideally, this list should be prepared by a committee of lighting designer, director, designer and the member of the stage management who will 'run' the show and call the cues. If the choreographer and costume designer have a strong contribution to make to the discussion they may wish to be present; otherwise they will delegate their representation to director and scene designer respectively.

If pressure of time prevents this meeting, the lighting designer should draw up a proposed list and circulate it for comment. Either way, before the first lighting rehearsal, it is essential that the cues be pencilled into the prompt copy. The importance of this should become apparent in later chapters.

RIGGING METHODS	Wherever possible, lighting instruments are fixed to horizontal or vertical alloy tubing with the external diameter of standard scaffolding. Horizontals are known as *bars* (*pipes* in America) and verticals as *booms*. Hook clamps and boom arms are designed to hang lights so that both instrument and lamp operate on their correct axis for maximum lamp life. Brackets are useful for temporary rigging of single lamps, particularly those hung from the timber of scenery flats, but their use is far too limiting for a permanent installation. For auditorium positions in particular, lengths of standard tubing give much more flexibility than brackets.
REHEARSING THE LIGHTS	The integration of the lighting fit-up with the scenery fit-up is discussed in the section of the book dealing with the details of the staging process for various types of production.
ELECTRICS POSTSCRIPT	Production lighting is not the only function of the electrics department. They provide lights for rehearsal pianos, production desks, music stands and quick-change rooms. They rig special cue lights and provide feeds for smoke guns. They deal with irons, washing machines, spinners, drying cabinets and the other modern aids to wardrobe and wig maintenance. They cope with actors' shavers, portable television sets and hairdryers. In all except the largest repertoire theatres, the production electricians double up as the building's maintenance staff. Allow for this in scheduling, and notify *all* foreseeable requirements in advance of the get-in.

8   Sound

Theatre sound technology has advanced to the point where it is no longer something superimposed during the dress rehearsals. Sound is an integral part of a stage presentation and it requires design.

SOUND DESIGNER   The person responsible for planning the sound is the sound designer. This job can be doubled with director, stage manager or sound operator, but in most productions there is quite enough work involved to keep one person fully employed on sound design alone. If the job is doubled, the person taking on the additional responsibility for sound design must understand the full extent of pre-planning required.

The sound designer has to be not only a mixture of artist and technician but a good chairman as well. Sound is not superimposed but distilled from the ideas of author, composer, director, designer and choreographer as well as sound designer. There is often a considerable degree of compromise involved and it is the sound designer who must resolve any conflicts of opinion among the production team, and evolve an acceptable unified concept that is capable of execution with the resources available.

If these words about the sound designer seem familiar, it is because they are identical with those about lighting designers in the previous chapter – the only change is the substitution of 'sound' for 'light'. The specialist sound designer is becoming accepted as an essential member of the production team.

THE ROLE OF SOUND   Electronically processed sound is used in the theatre for three purposes: the *reinforcement* of the level of vocal and instrumental sound produced by the performers, the addition of *sound effects*, and for *communications.*

SOUND REINFORCEMENT   Reinforcement of the level of sound is not just a matter of the degree of amplification, it is a positive component of production style. 'How are we going to use sound?' must be an early question in production planning. It is a question that should surface from time to time as the director and production team work out their concept prior to the commencement of rehearsals.

The decision may well be to use no sound reinforcement. This is fine, provided it is a deliberate, conscious decision made only after considera- tion of the theatre's acoustics and the actors' projection ability. If the sound is to be reinforced, it can be done *subconsciously, consciously* or as an *intrinsic* production technique.

Subconscious reinforcement

Audiences have become accustomed to higher sound levels than for- merly. Radio, television and audio recordings in the home tend to be adjusted to levels sufficiently high to make concentration unnecessary for listening. Cinema has helped the process and the gradual introduc- tion of more and more sound reinforcement into the theatre has brought the average audience to the point where they no longer expect to have to make any sort of active effort to hear.

Correct sound levels are a vital component of the actor–audience relationship. To make contact with their audience, actors must be clearly heard, yet an excess volume of sound can act as a barrier. Perhaps the way to find the ideal level is to cut back to the point where the audience are on the point of having to concentrate. This threshold of concentration is considerably louder than the threshold of audibility.

Reinforcement is not normally required for speech in theatres which have been built specifically as playhouses. These include the smaller auditoria of the old traditional theatre centres like Broadway and the London West End, together with the smaller, say up to about seven or eight hundred seater, regional theatres built specifically for the spoken word in the last forty years. The acoustic of the large mixed-programme houses, built fifty-plus years ago when touring was at its height, may be able to handle Shakespearean productions on an epic scale. However, intimate drama is likely to require some reinforcement used as discreetly as possible so that the audience are not too consciously aware of it.

This requires discreet positioning of microphones. In old horseshoe theatres with a relatively narrow proscenium opening (certainly not more than 30 ft) it may be possible to use long range 'gun' microphones on the box fronts nearest to the stage, but normally a series of 'float mikes' along the front edge of the stage will be required. The latest designs have small heads on slender columns so that they are relatively unobtrusive. Radio microphones concealed in the actors' clothing, although acceptable in a musical show, tend to bring the sound of a straight play to a level which strains the credibility of any attempt at naturalism in the acting.

The discreet placement of microphones is not the only feature of subconscious reinforcement. The primary source must appear to be the actors rather than the loudspeakers. This obviously requires particularly high quality equipment and the use of a relatively low level of amplification. In this way some resemblance of a logical relationship can be maintained between the level of sound and the distance between speaker and listener.

Opera is probably the one form of theatre that rarely needs reinforcement – with the possible exception of the continuo harpsichord when chamber opera is played in a large house designed for romantic opera. However, with louder and louder stereophony and quadrophony in the home, it could well come to pass that a future generation of opera buffs might demand that their live opera performances be reinforced to reach the level which can be produced by a high gain sound reproducer in a small room.

Conscious reinforcement

In musicals there is now very rarely any attempt to apply a discreet reinforcement of which the audience will only be aware at a sub-conscious level. Radio microphones concealed in costumes or wigs are standard, while other microphones are prominently in view and the sound is amplified to a level which it would be difficult to ignore. In 'light entertainment', the modern descendant of the music hall and variety stages where personality performers work directly to the audience, the microphone can become a vital prop and its handling a carefully rehearsed and essential part of the performer's technique. Indeed the handling of the microphone can be made so much a conscious part of the production style that radio microphones are often handled as props rather than concealed in costumes.

Intrinsic reinforcement

For many forms of modern music, the studio recording rather than the written score has become the definitive form of publication. The music only exists when the individual vocal and instrumental threads have been electronically processed. Although tempo and phrasing remain the responsibility of the conductor in the orchestra pit, control of balance has been handed over to the sound operator at the mixer.

This approach is now applied to the writing of stage musicals. In many cases the recording appears first. Its success may provide the stimulus for mounting a stage production or the recording may be part of the wider marketing strategy for a show for which there is already a production commitment. In such circumstances the theatre sound quality must strive to match that of the studio recording. To do this the sound becomes an intrinsic part of the production with each vocal and instrumental part separately picked up by its own microphone and balanced through a multi-channel mixer of studio proportions. Sound assumes a major role in the budget and becomes so fundamental that it is probably no longer correct to talk of it as mere reinforcement.

Taped vocals

It is difficult to sing well while dancing an energetically choreographed chorus routine. One solution is to dance to a playback of tape-recorded song. To add to the realism, the dancers try to sing a bit rather than just mime and the orchestra accompaniment is live. To ensure synchronisation, a twin track tape is used, with the second track (the 'click track') feeding the beat through headsets to the conductor and rhythm players in the orchestra. Cueing of the tape at the start of each sequence requires critical timing and the usual method is to have a remote start button on the conductor's music stand in the pit. As a precaution against breakdown, the bigger shows also have a stand-by tape running in synchronisation with the main tape. Carefully used, the technique can be made to look plausible, but it suffers from a major drawback: the tape sets an inflexible timing and it is subtle variations in timing that make a live show live. The real solution to vocals in dance numbers is to have a group of 'pit singers' as members of the orchestra. But this is expensive.

Foldback

All the sound reinforcement discussed above has been for the benefit of the audience and the loudspeakers have been directed towards them. In many circumstances, sound reinforcement has to be directed towards

Foldback loudspeaker mounted backstage to help the actors hear themselves and their accompaniment.

the actors from on-stage loudspeakers. This is called *foldback* and is a separate mix from that fed to the audience. In reinforced shows (particularly those with conscious reinforcement) actors usually need foldback not only to hear their accompaniment but also to hear their own voices at a sufficiently high level to give them confidence that they are being heard by the audience. In opera, although there is no reinforcement for the audience, some foldback from the pit is often required to let singers hear their accompaniment and pick up note pitches.

Audience reaction reinforcement

All the increase in performance sound levels can make applause, laughter and general audience reaction 'buzz' seem quiet by comparison. This could be detrimental to that audience communal feeling which is an essential part of the actor–audience relationship. There is therefore a case for giving the audience some foldback of their own reactions. When this technique is used, it is done with considerable discretion because there are those who might consider the amplification of applause or laughter to be cheating.

SOUND EQUIPMENT

Mixers

The heart of a reinforcement installation is the *mixer* where the inputs from the various microphones are balanced and routed to the appropriate loudspeakers. There is a parallel between sound mixing desks and lighting control desks in that both function by balancing the relative levels of the various input channels (indeed the term 'light mixer' would probably be a more appropriate term than the customary 'lighting control' or 'board').

The key component in any sound channel is therefore the *fader* for controlling the level at which that channel's microphone contributes to the mix. In early mixers the fader was a rotary control ('pot') and may occasionally still be so in the very simplest inexpensive models. In mixers of the standard desirable for professional theatre use, however, the fader is a linear slider which is easier to read – both at a glance and by feel. To allow the full travel of the fader to be used, there is often a channel *sensitivity* control which sets the maximum level of its channel. This spreads the available range of travel from zero to agreed maximum, across the whole length of the fader. By limiting the maximum level, the channel can be operated without risk of going into the high pitched squeal of howlround (often called 'feedback').

Unlike a lighting desk, a sound mixer desk controls quality as well as quantity. Each channel has *equalisation* controls to adjust tonal quality. It is usual to find a minimum of three rotary pots for equalisation, giving cut or boost to the *treble, mid* and *bass* frequency bands. For comparison of the processed tonal quality with the original non-equalised sound, there should be an *equalisation cut* switch.

Sound mixing desk   A *PFL* (*pre-fade-listen*) switch allows the operator to check in advance
(Allen & Heath GL4   that the channel is working or that an off-stage actor is standing by.
by Harmon Audio)   Auxiliary controls are likely to include facilities for *foldback* (at a level
                         either subject to the channel faders or independent of them) and
                         facilities for introducing optional *echo* into the channel. Finally there
                         are routing controls to allow the channels to be grouped with other
                         channels under the overall control of master faders. The mixer feeds the
                         power amplifiers and there are further controls to route the output to
                         the appropriate loudspeakers.

                             In a big musical with individual channels for virtually every singer
                         and musician, the operator can have an awful lot of pots to control.
                         Small wonder, therefore, that there is an increasing use of computer
                         memory to carry out some of the routing operations so that the
                         operator's hands and mind are free to concentrate on the fader levels
                         which require subtle balancing that varies from one performance to
                         another.

Microphones   There are two types of microphone in standard use for sound reinforce-
                         ment in theatres: *dynamic* and *condenser*. Although dynamic micro-
                         phones are more robust, the condenser types give higher quality (and
                         consequently are more expensive), but need more careful handling.

Condenser mikes are normally used for the main pick-up positions, particularly floats, with dynamic mikes in subsidiary positions.

Some microphones (sometimes called 'non-directional' but more properly *omni-directional*) are equally sensitive in picking up sound from all directions. Others are only sensitive in certain directions. One type, often known as *figure-of-eight*, is sensitive to the front and rear but insensitive to the sides. The most useful types for theatre are *cardioid* (directional) and *hyper-cardioid* (very directional). These have heart shaped pick-up patterns which are extremely sensitive to the front but virtually dead to the sides and rear. This enables the microphone to be 'focused' on the desired part of the stage action and, because the dead sides are towards the loudspeakers, there is a diminished risk of picking up the sound from these loudspeakers and developing howlround. Some condenser mikes have variable directional qualities. The most directional pick-up is from gun microphones (sometimes called 'rifles') but, while they are undoubtedly very useful at up to about three times the range of a normal cardioid, they are not miracle workers. They will not, alas, pick up the actors and ignore the orchestra when fixed to a balcony some forty feet from stage and pit.

At the other extreme, microphones attached to the actor, whether hung around the neck on cords, clipped to the costume or hidden in the wig, have to be omni-directional. To allow freedom of movement, these microphones usually feed their signal to a separate small radio transmitter concealed within the costume.

The development of radio microphones has virtually ended the use, even for variety, revue and pantomime, of riser microphones which could pop up through traps in the stage floor to the appropriate height required by the performer.

LOUDSPEAKERS   Whereas microphones convert sound into electrical energy, loudspeakers convert the electrical impulses back into sound – after they have been processed in the mixer and magnified in the power amplifiers. Just as microphones have to be directional in picking up the actors, so too must the loudspeakers be directional in distributing the sound to the audience. A directional loudspeaker system not only directs the sound towards the audience, it ensures that the amplified sound is not fed back in any quantity to the stage where it would be picked up again by the microphones to produce howlround. What we commonly refer to as loudspeakers are in fact two-part: the actual loudspeaker units and their housings or cabinets for which the proper word is *enclosures.*

There are two kinds of loudspeakers used in theatre work: *line source* and *horn.* The *line source* has a column of separate cone loudspeakers mounted vertically in a long slender enclosure. The directional effect of doing this is to restrict the vertical coverage and increase the horizontal

The Bose system (*right*) allows even distribution of the full frequency range from a compact enclosure. Note, also, the 'show relay' microphone feeding performance sound to the dressing rooms.

Small loudspeakers (*below*) mounted under the overhang of a balcony allow the reinforced sound to the rear seats to be delayed to coincide with the natural sound.

coverage of the sound. In the highest quality models there are separate columns of high and low frequency cones in the same enclosure. Mounted near the proscenium arch, they help maintain the illusion that the sound is coming from the stage. They can be angled so that they give a wide horizontal coverage of the audience yet do not blast the people in the front rows who will receive sound from only the lowest speakers in the column. These line source speakers are reasonably elegant and do not conflict unduly with theatre auditorium architecture. They are therefore useful for subconscious reinforcement.

As the sound becomes a more dominant feature of production style or the auditorium becomes particularly large, it is necessary to move into loudspeaker types which, although more physically obtrusive, have improved frequency response and power output. These use a combination of high frequency *horn* units and separate bass horns in chunky enclosures designed to enhance bass response.

Wiring

The microphones, mixers, amplifiers and loudspeakers in the sound chain have to be linked by wiring. The growth of sound has been so fast that much permanent wiring has become obsolescent almost as soon as installed. The very nature of an adaptable sound system implies considerable temporary wiring but, with a good permanent installation, the temporary runs can be kept reasonably short. The whole process relies on a high quality standardised plug and socket interconnection system. This whole subject is beyond the scope of this book and we can only entreat anyone responsible for specifying sound wiring to 'think big' and to study appropriate recommendations – in Britain, for example, the sound wiring recommendations published by the Association of British Theatre Technicians.

Sound control position

In older theatres the termination point for microphone and speaker lines was usually adjacent to the prompt corner. In new and refurbished theatres the lines all go to jack fields in a sound control room forming part of the lighting, sound and projection suite at the rear of the auditorium. The sound control room usually contains effects tape decks in addition to the mixer. For productions making any considerable use of reinforcement, however, there is a very strong case for the mixer being in the auditorium so that the operator can balance live rather than through a window or by monitor loudspeakers. Certainly, such a position has to be available for certain types of shows and any serious upgrading of a theatre's technical installation should include provision for seat removal and access to tie-lines.

SOUND EFFECTS

Sound effects can be live, reinforced-live, or taped. The choice, once again, is a matter of production style.

Temporary sound
mixing position in the
auditorium

Live effects

Over the centuries, prior to the availability of electronically processed sound, the theatre has developed methods of producing realistic effects on cue. Coconut shells for horses' hooves is probably the effect that has most caught the public imagination and any sensitive theatre worker must have an occasional nostalgic yearning for the days when a storm could command an orchestra of wind machines, rain machines, drums ad lib plus sinister rumblings from a series of cannon balls rolling through a permanent thunder run in the upper regions of the stage and possibly above the auditorium as well. Apart from any other considerations, such complex sequences are now usually ruled out by the large number of operators required. However, for simpler effects like door slams and glass crashes, the old live way is probably still the best.

**Reinforced live
effects**

If the actors' voices are being reinforced, any live effects will probably require to be reinforced as well, partly to make them loud enough and partly to give them the same tonal quality as the voices. The effect is performed to a microphone and an appropriately positioned loud-speaker produces the sound from the logical direction.

Taped effects

Most sound effects are now inserted in the performance by replaying a specially edited tape. Reel-to-reel machines rather than cassettes are used, for simplified editing and accurate cueing. Where possible, the effects are arranged in sequence on a single tape with short coloured leaders between each cue. On older machines, metal foils were used to

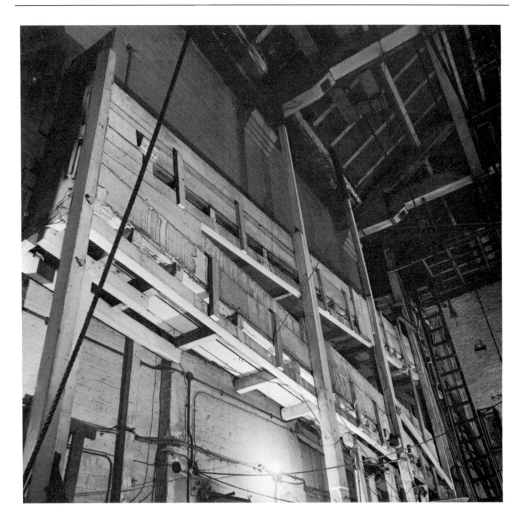

The nineteenth-century thunder run at Her Majesty's Theatre in London. Tape recordings are now usually used for such effects.

line up the next cue automatically but most decks now use clear tape with a photo cell.

If the effects plot is very complex there may be an overlap of various sounds, and this overlap may vary from night to night due to the timing variations that are the inevitable and characteristic feature of a live stage performance. To cope with this, theatres normally use twin track machines. Different effects can be recorded on each track to be mixed as desired during replay. Many theatre installations include two twin track machines and this gives enough flexibility for the average production; 7½ inches per second is the standard speed used.

An alternative method is to use *Cart* (cartridge) machines where each effect is recorded on its own dedicated tape cartridge.

If a movement of sound from one part of the stage to another is required, the effect can be 'panned' (i.e., crossfaded) from one loud-speaker to another: this provides more precise control of the performance timing of the sound's movement than if it were recorded in stereo with a fixed timing.

Specific effects may be obtained from a sound library and/or they may be recorded specially. Recording of the 'real' sound seldom works: as in the case of live effects, a faked sound often has more realism. Specialist books on sound give some useful starting hints but one should allow time for recording experiments. Fortunately tape can be wiped and re-used.

COMMUNICATIONS Communication between technicians during performances is now carried out almost entirely by voice. In simple shows, cue lights may still be used to signal flys and other backstage positions but voice is invariably used for electrics (board and follow spots). Cue lights are still installed in these positions but are only intended for emergency use in the event of a breakdown in the sound network. The basic method of sound communication is by ring intercom.

Ring intercom It is now standard to have a wire loop linking all technical areas. At key positions there are socket boxes into which a headset may be plugged to allow that position to talk and listen to everyone else using the loop. Each headset is fed through a belt pack which has a push button and call light to attract attention plus a key switch to talk. There are often two channels to separate, say, electrics traffic from the rest. These ring intercom headsets known as 'cans' have become the standard method for stage managers to call cues.

MIDI Because subtle variations in timing from one performance to the next are the essence of what makes a live show live, it is inevitable that the verbal calling of cues will remain a feature of stage productions. However, digital technology in the form of *MIDI* (acronym for Musical Instrument Digital Interface) offers the possibility of integrating the cues of all the different control systems so that a single event, such as a quaver in the music, triggers a sequence of actions involving sound, light and scenic movement. It seems likely that we shall see a growing use of this type of technology to integrate cue sequences, although the triggering event will be one which is dependent upon the performers' timing response to a particular audience.

Inductive loops It is possible to run a loop aerial around the building so that technicians can carry small radio receivers with ear-pieces of the deaf-aid type. Unfortunately, the amount of steelwork in a modern theatre acts as a screen, making reception uncertain in important areas like bridges and understage. These inductive loops have been used successfully to cue technicians driving trucked scenery with complex movements and, in a dire emergency, could be used for prompting.

Infra-red

The use of inductive loops for reinforcing sound for the members of the audience with impaired hearing has now been superseded by infra-red systems. These are also used for relaying simultaneous translation of foreign language plays to individual members of the audience.

Radio microphones

Radio microphones are useful for focusing lights. The lighting designer has to move all over the stage while calling channel numbers to the switchboard and giving instructions to electricians who may be on distant bridges. A radio microphone feeding into the communication system gives freedom of movement and is particularly useful in repertoire theatres where refocusing of spotlights may be required during scene changes.

Production desk

Communication facilities are required for rehearsals at the production desk position in the auditorium. The lighting designer requires a set of cans and provision should be made for the director to speak to the cast in a show of any size, although this can be a little tricky to arrange in a musical without introducing howlround.

Dressing room calls

Dressing room loudspeakers are fed with two programmes: show relay and stage management calls. When calls are being given, the show relay is automatically cancelled. A knob on each speaker allows the volume of the show relay to be adjusted, but this does not affect calls. There is usually a subsidiary microphone in the stage door keeper's office but this is automatically overridden by the call key on the prompt desk microphone.

Telephones

In a theatre of any size there will be an internal administrative telephone network with key technical areas included. When these telephones are within sound of the stage or auditorium they should have a flashing light as an alternative to the normal bell.

Closed circuit video

Most theatres have a video camera in the auditorium to relay the show to the prompt desk and to latecomers waiting to take their seats in a suitable pause. Increasingly, theatres are installing dressing room monitors which can be switched to broadcast television channels or to the picture of the stage. In opera houses there is always a camera in the pit to relay the conductor's beat to the off-stage areas.

Audience calls

New installations include loudspeakers in audience circulation areas such as foyers and bars so that – as an alternative or addition to traditional bells – the stage manager can call the audience ('Ladies and Gentlemen, the curtain will rise in one minute', etc.).

Contact

Having stressed the need for good communications, it may seem perverse to go on to warn against too much of it. But there is a danger – particularly with the wearing of 'cans' – that the technical staff may get so involved in communicating that they lose contact with the show. Technicians, like actors, are not robots: without in any way departing from the details of the rehearsal framework, there is scope for subtle variations in timing. To be alive to this, the technician must be in contact (which is not quite the same as merely listening) with the show rather than cocooned in a communications network. One ear for the show, the other for the SM? This is not an easy point to make – it is all part of that indefinable 'What makes a live show live?'.

ORGANISATION

To ensure the most efficient use of limited staging time, the sound department requires considerable advance planning. The amount of planning will vary with the type of production and the type of producing organisation. A company performing in its own theatre will probably have a comprehensive sound system, in which case planning will be mainly preparing tapes and deciding if any microphones or loudspeakers need to be repositioned. At the other extreme, a musical moving into a rented theatre may have to plan to hire and install every single item down to the last piece of cable.

Planning can be carried out under the headings already discussed in this chapter:

Reinforcement planning requires the preparation of detailed drawings showing microphone types and positions, speaker types and positions, and the assignment of mixer channels.

Effects planning starts from an acquisition list of effects. After editing, the tape should be played during the final run-throughs in the rehearsal room to check on cue positions, length, etc.

Communications planning requires decisions on the outstations required for stage management cueing in performance, together with an assessment of extra communication facilities required for the technical and dress rehearsal period.

9   Wardrobe

There was once a production of 'The Clandestine Marriage' where the director shouted in the middle of the tech: 'Stop, stop, hold it . . . either we remake all the costumes or we widen all the doors.' This was, of course, an exaggeration and nothing drastic was done to either the doors or the costumes. The actors just had to make less than perfect exits and entrances for the next three months. It was sad that such a situation – doors narrowed for perspective, and skirt fullness increased for effect – should reach the final production weekend before discovery. More common is the impossible quick change which entails frantic alterations at the last minute. Yes, it's back to our old friend *planning*!

DESIGN

As with the other staging departments, our concern here is not with costume design but with wardrobe organisation: not the internal wardrobe organisation concerned with the cutting and making of costumes, but the organisation by which the wardrobe department integrates with everyone else. Nevertheless, design is never just a matter of visual aesthetics and so there are a number of design practicalities to be raised and got out of the way at early production conferences.

In particular, before a costume design is approved by the director, there has to be consideration of whether the actor can work in it. Singing and dancing can be difficult, if not impossible, in certain styles of costume and the designer will need to know if the actor is going to be called upon to do any complex movement.

Incidentally, the door problem mentioned above occurred in a production where there were separate designers for settings and costumes. In such circumstances the director and production manager need to keep an eye and an ear on the design partnership, ever ready to detect a lack of harmony not just over practical matters, but possibly over fundamentals like style and colour as well.

COSTUME SUPERVISOR

The key organisational person is the Costume Supervisor. The duties may be carried out by the head of the wardrobe department in a

(*left*) Costume design
by Theodor Pitsek

producing theatre. For companies without their own theatre or wardrobe department, the duties may be carried out by the production's wardrobe mistress. But the work load is usually more than sufficient to justify recruiting a freelance for the production period through to the opening performance. Liaising between costume designer and costume suppliers, the Costume Supervisor ensures that all the clothes are ready on schedule and within budget. Apart from a comprehensive knowledge of costuming and an eye for accurate detail, the job demands considerable management skills, particularly in handling actors and boosting their confidence.

WARDROBE PLOT

The wardrobe plot is an actor-by-actor, scene-by-scene inventory of all the costumes in a production. It is a detailed breakdown which lists every separate item in each costume. It serves as a checklist during budgeting, making, fittings, and when the clothes are packed and unpacked. Director and choreographer have copies so that they know how individual chorus members will be dressed in any particular scene. This will affect grouping and choreographic patterns, so the director and choreographer need to know who is wearing what. The stage management also has a copy and it can be useful if they provide labels for the first blocking rehearsals. Incidentally, this is a good moment for the stage management to exercise their characteristic tact and develop a friendly relationship with the acting company. Most people do not really like having labels stuck on them but with an explanation and joke from the production and stage management teams all will be well and indeed, with the right approach, the chorus will be made to feel like individuals.

MAKING

Whether costumes are made 'in house' in the theatre's own workrooms or whether they are made by outside contractors will depend on the type of production company mounting the show. Only companies with their own theatres or companies presenting long regular seasons in rented theatres are likely to have their own workrooms, and these workrooms are often concerned more with alterations to accommodate cast changes in revivals of old productions than in making for new productions. Even the biggest repertoire organisations are likely to have some of their costumes made 'out' – very often it is the highly specialised men's tailoring that is contracted out.

HIRING

For short runs, costumes may be rented under various arrangements between the extremes of everything being selected from existing stock, or everything made specially and then absorbed into the costumier's

A wardrobe plot

```
'ROBINSON CRUSOE' THEATRE ROYAL/NEWCASTLE


COSTUME PLOT


ACT ONE    PROLOGUE

BLACKBEARD                        Black Velvet Coat trimmed Gold Braid,
                                  Black Shirt, Breeches, Belt, Boots,
                                  Gloves, Black Hat with Skull and Cross-
                                  bones, Red Cloak with Skull and Cross-
                                  bones, Red Kerchief for head, Black
                                  Kerchief for neck, Earrings, Chains.


FAIRY                             Green Lurex Leotard, Silk Chiffon Drapes
                                  in shades of green, Tiara, Pink Tights,
                                  Ballet Pointes or Green Court Shoes.


ACT ONE    SCENE 1                THE HARBOUR OF WHITLEY BAY

GIRL DANCERS                  (1) Fishergirl Dresses in various colours
                                  with White Petticoats attached, coloured
                                  Kerchiefs for necks, White Briefs,
                                  White Tights, Black Buckle Shoes.

                              (2) Red and White Striped Tee-Shirts, White
                                  Trousers, Black Belts, Black Sailor Hats,
                                  Tights and Shoes as above, Navy Blue Short
                                  Jackets, Red Kerchiefs.


4  BOY SINGERS AND                Red and White Tee-Shirts, White Trousers,
1 EXTRA COSTUME                   Black Belts, Black Sailor Hats or Wool
                                  Caps, White Socks, Black Buckle Shoes,
                                  Navy Blue Jackets, Red Kerchiefs.


CRUSOE                            Navy Blue Jacket, Gold Briefs, Tan Tights,
                                  Black Court Shoes, Lace Jabot and Cuffs.


POLLY                             Purple Velvet Bodice with White Organdie
                                  Skirt decorated with Yellow Daisies,
                                  White Petticoat attached, Yellow Briefs,
                                  Tan Tights, Yellow Shoes, Yellow Hat,
                                  Mauve Gloves.


MOTHER RILEY                      Own Costume.
```

rental stock at the end of the run. There is a whole range of compromises between these extremes: decision will depend on budget and that elusive hunt for the most cost-effective way of spending the allocated money.

REHEARSAL COSTUMES

An actress in a full hooped skirt takes up more stage space than an actress in rehearsal jeans: there are restrictions on her movements and

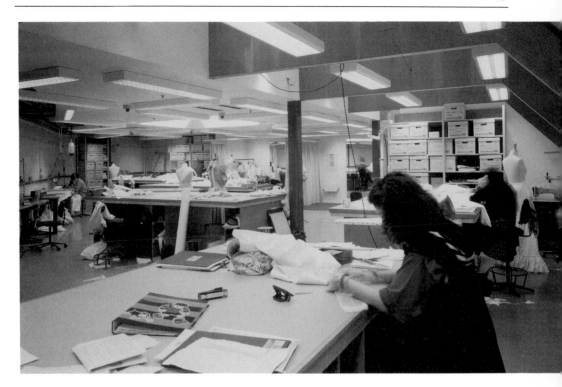

The costume work-shop at West Yorkshire Playhouse.

her relations with other members of the cast. It is therefore useful – and the practice in most opera companies particularly – to make petticoats of suitable fullness available in the rehearsal room. Hats can be tricky and it is useful for them to be available in advance of the final dress rehearsal period.

FITTING

Costume fittings are tricky to schedule. Costume making is invariably carried out against the clock and so once a costume has reached the point where a fitting is required, it is important to get actor, designer, cutter and costume together as soon as possible. In most productions there is a concentrated rehearsal period of three to five weeks with rehearsal sessions each and every day. Removing actors for fittings – usually at short notice – can play havoc with rehearsal schedules, particularly at the later stages of rehearsals when the play is being 'run' in longish sections.

Scheduling fittings is a little easier in repertoire theatres. Rehearsal periods are spread over a longer period with shorter daily sessions and so it is simpler to arrange fittings without removing actors from the rehearsal room. There can, however, be problems in opera houses where costumes sometimes have to be made to dubious measurements sent by post. The singer may then have to be rushed straight from airport to wardrobe.

An actor's first encounter with an unfinished costume can be a touch neurotic and this is understandable. If leads are being asked to wear designs in which they are thought to lack complete confidence, it is a good policy for the director to attend the first fitting to spread confidence.

GETTING IN

Production companies with their own theatres have all the necessary wardrobe equipment installed on a permanent basis and when such companies work in repertoire, there is an organisational framework to get the right costume to the right dressing room on the right day. A company going into a rented theatre, however, has to organise a 'get-in'. In addition to transporting costumes to the theatre, it may be necessary to take in costume rails with dust sheets plus such standard items of wardrobe maintenance as washing machines, driers, irons, ironing boards, sewing machines, etc. It is sensible (but not always done) to check in advance that the electrical equipment has the right plugs.

DRESS PARADES

On the day of the first rehearsal in costume, or if possible on a day previous, it is usual and useful to hold a dress parade where all members of the cast put on each of their costumes in sequence and parade before director and designer together with the senior members of the team who have been responsible for cutting and making. Whenever possible the dress parade is held on the stage so that the clothes can be seen at a distance and under stage lighting conditions. The dress parade is a chance to see the exact state of wardrobe preparation and detailed lists are prepared of missing items and alterations required. It is also a good moment to check such things as the matching of chorus groups. And anyone who thinks that they may have a movement or breathing problem will be quite vociferous about it at this time.

DRESS REHEARSALS

At dress rehearsals, especially the first one, it is essential that the Costume Supervisor sits with the production team in the auditorium to take notes and to discuss with the director and designer any costume problems as they occur. If wardrobe preparations are behind, it is very tempting for all the wardrobe staff to be upstairs working on the uncompleted costumes. But this is a temptation to be resisted: if costumes are incomplete, it is particularly important for a senior person to be present to check that the missing items are in fact being made and to reassure everyone of that fact. With the possible exception of the very first rehearsals in costume, the dressers should always be present as for performance.

QUICK CHANGES   When simple quick changes are to be done in the wings, the dresser stands by with the change of clothes, helps the actor, then takes the discarded costume back to the dressing room. If the actor is going to drop any garments, the dresser should lay out a dust sheet on the stage floor to catch these. A few theatres have permanent quick change rooms adjacent to the stage. Mostly, however, a complex quick change involves improvising a temporary room in a corner of the stage from scenery flats with chair, table, mirror, lights and probably a dress rail.

DRESS   Dress rehearsals are the moment to instil costume discipline: no eating
REHEARSAL   in costume, no sitting in the auditorium, etc. Technical stage work
COSTUME CARE   continues to be in progress between dress rehearsals: the stage floor may not therefore always be quite as clean as it will be at performance. To protect long dresses, it is useful to tack polythene over the lower few inches which will be in contact with the floor.

WARDROBE   Visually, nothing lets a show down quite so much as badly looked after
MAINTENANCE   costumes. The clean crisp look will help blind the audience to deficiencies in other areas, including many shortcomings in the actual design of the costumes. Even clothes that are intended to look dirty and crumpled must be cleaned and pressed. Any dirt and crumple should arise from design not from lack of care. Wardrobe maintenance is like any other maintenance: routine planned overhauls in an attempt to avoid or at least minimise breakdowns. This means scheduling laundry, cleaning and pressing on a regular basis, coupled with actors' and dressers' co-operation in drawing the wardrobe staff's attention to the need for minor repairs as soon as that need arises.

WIGS   In opera and classical drama companies there is a separate wig department: otherwise wigs and hair pieces come under the umbrella of the wardrobe department. There is nothing quite so eye-catching as a badly dressed wig and so, unless the production uses enough wigs to justify a specialist on the staff, arrangements must be made for the wigs to be returned to a perruquier for regular dressing.

Part III

THE STAGING PROCESS

10   Staging the Play

Now let us follow the staging of a play from the point where it gets possession of the stage until it opens to the public for performance. Let us assume that it is a play being produced for a 'run', rather than a play being slotted into a repertoire. Let us take as our starting point the state of preparation that the play should be in when it reaches its final run-through in the rehearsal room.

The *actors* will have developed to the pitch where they can go no further without the supporting environment of scenery, costumes, props, effects, music and lights. Indeed the acting intensity will now drop temporarily while they adjust to coping with the technicalities of the stage apparatus. Then the acting will start to rise again, now integrated with the staging, until the production reaches the pitch where it can go no further without an audience. Building a company of actors to the right pitch at the right time, not too early and not too late, is a basic skill of the good director.

The *stage management* will have the prompt book absolutely up to date with all cues and warnings marked in as far as known. They will have double-checked on the state of preparations in the various departments and where they foresee snags they will have quietly prepared contingency plans, 'just in case'. Numbers of staff required for fit-up, rehearsals and performances will have been agreed with the departmental heads and the appropriate calls made. In the event of unforeseen circumstances playing havoc with the schedule, they will have checked the movements (in terms of telephone numbers) of all actors and staging personnel up to the time of their first 'call' on stage. They will have satisfied themselves that everyone has received and understood the schedule and they will have ensured that there is an ample stock of coffee, tea, milk and sugar to sustain themselves and their fellow workers in the hours ahead.

The *scenery* will be completely constructed and painted. It will be fitted with all necessary cleats, lines, pin hinges, hanging irons, etc. If the workshop is big enough there will have been a trial set-up of sections, if not of the whole set. Edges of flattage or framed borders which show to the audience will not have been forgotten in the painting and, where the lighting plan shows that light is likely to bleed through the canvas, the back of that canvas will have been painted opaque. Hanging wire, timber battening, hinge-pins, screws, screw-eyes, nuts, bolts and any other necessary ironmongery items will be ready – together with the tools to use them. All items of scenery will be marked in a way that corresponds to the stage and hanging plans. Scene change and fly plots will have been prepared and agreed with the stage management.

All *props* will have been made or selected. The smaller items will have been in use for the final days in the rehearsal room. Arrangements will have been made for a supply of expendable props such as food, drinks and smokes. A sufficient number of disposable items like letters for tearing up and crocks for breaking will have been prepared for the period up to and a little beyond the opening night. All props will be check listed and plots prepared.

The *electrics* department will have prepared the lighting equipment required by the lighting design plan, with additional equipment being hired where necessary. Cables will have the correct plugs and will be in appropriate lengths. Multicores or taped-up cable ropes will have been prepared for feeding bars. Accessories will be standing by and all colour filters will be cut to size. Non-production lighting items like cue lights, working lights, motors, wardrobe equipment, etc., will be prepared. The lighting designer will have a cue synopsis agreed with director, designer and stage manager.

The *sound* tapes will be prepared and the principal effects should have been tried out in the rehearsal room. Equipment will be ready, including kit for editing. The theatre's communication equipment will have been investigated and any necessary modifications such as extra outstations ordered. Planned intercom facilities will include the production desk in the auditorium.

The *wardrobe* will have had their final fittings and the clothes will be ready to wear. The theatre's wardrobe maintenance equipment will have been appraised and any necessary additions ordered.

All this may seem like an impossible ideal, but it has to be our target.

SCHEDULING   Unless the play is particularly complicated, the maximum time likely to be available in a touring theatre will be from after the get-out of the previous show on Saturday night/Sunday morning until curtain up on Tuesday. This means about 65 hours, or for a Monday opening about 40 hours. In a regional producing theatre, there may be a further day. Because all these hours exist, there is a temptation to feel that they should all be worked. But night work leads to decreasing efficiency on the following day and certainly no one should ever be asked (or allowed) to work two consecutive nights while continuing by day. The two

schedules shown here illustrate the sort of proportioning of time that
has been found practical for simple and not-quite-so-simple plays.

```
SUNDAY
  8.00              Get-in & fit-up
13.00 - 14.00       Lunch
14.00 - 18.00       Focus lights & plot cues.  Dress set.
18.00 - 18.30       Break
18.45 - 23.00       Technical dress rehearsal

MONDAY
  9.00 - 13.00      Technical work on stage
12.30               Cast for notes in stalls bar
13.00 - 14.00       Lunch
14.15               Dress Rehearsal
19.40               Press photo on stage
20.00               First performance
```

(above) Typical schedule for a simple play

```
SUNDAY
01.00               Get-in & commence fit-up (stage + electrics)

10.00               Commence focusing (1 flyman standing by)
                    Stage continue building trucks in dock

12.00 - 13.00       Stage lunch break

13.00 - 14.00       Electrics lunch break

14.00               Complete focusing

15.00 approx        Commence plotting

18.00 - 19.00       Stage & electrics supper break
                    Director set sound levels

19.15               Act I Tech (costume, no make-up)

23.00               Finish

MONDAY
08.00 - 12.00       Technical work as required

12.00 - 13.00       Crew lunch
                    Cast Photocall

13.00 - 18.15       Act II Tech (costume, no make-up)

19.25               Half-hour call for Dress Rehearsal

20.00               Full Dress Rehearsal

23.00               Finish (Stage free for painters)

TUESDAY
08.00 - 13.00       Technical work as required

13.00               Company for notes in stalls
                    (Stage available from 13.00)

13.00 - 14.00       Crew lunch

14.15               Dress Rehearsal (no make-up)

19.30               First Peformance
```

(right) Typical schedule for a more complex play

UNLOADING

An efficient get-in begins with planned unloading. The basic aim is to
avoid double handling wherever possible: as each item is removed from
the truck it should be carried directly to a position on the stage as close
as possible to where it will be required. Wardrobe baskets and dress
rails are, naturally, taken straight to the wardrobe and if the stage is
particularly small or the play particularly large, it may be desirable to 'lay
off' certain items which are not required until a late point in the fit-up –
let's hope that there is a roomy scene dock or that there is an alleyway
and the sun is shining. Let's hope that the sun is shining anyway, for
very few get-ins are under cover. If there is an apron stage it may prove a
useful dumping ground for lighting equipment and/or bulky furniture.
Modern theatres often have a motorised orchestra pit which doubles as
an apron: it is worthwhile bringing this up to stage level for the period of
the fit-up. Flats which have been stowed on their sides in the van should

be raised upright as they are brought in, and should be stacked against the wall so that the first items required are not buried at the bottom of the pack. To make all this happen, the master carpenter in charge of the fit-up should stand on stage and assign a position to every item as it is carried in.

HANGING

Ideally the lighting equipment is rigged before the scenic fit-up starts, but frequently the lighting rigging and scenic fit-up are carried out simultaneously. This calls for careful integration. It is logical for both departments to start by hanging all their flown stuff and this usually works, if the stage staff start upstage and the electrics downstage. Once the lighting bars are flown, the electrics can move to the side of the stage to prepare booms, etc., and into the auditorium to work on FOH.

Lighting bars rigged at stage level and ready to be flown.

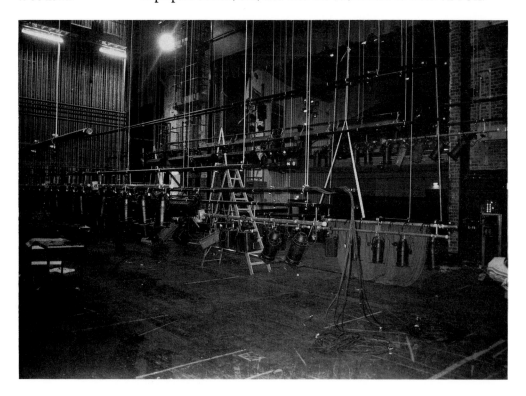

SETTING LINE

Scenery is positioned on the stage with reference to the *centre line* and the *setting line*. The centre line is (or should be) obvious but do not assume that it coincides with the middle of the centre aisle in the auditorium: old theatre architecture is often considerably off-centre. The centre line should be permanently marked at the front of the stage, on the stage side of the fire curtain, on every bar of the flying system and on the back wall. The setting line runs parallel to the front of the stage and its position will have been decided on the ground plans in advance. After it has been struck (usually with a chalked line), the company stage manager and lighting designer should confer with the master carpenter to ensure that there will be no problems arising from setting furniture upstage of the house curtain or in lighting from the theatre's fixed positions. These matters will (or should) have been considered in the early planning discussions but there are aspects of theatre architecture that do not show up clearly on theatre plans and sections, even when these are accurate and up to date. The actors and their director usually wish to set as far downstage as possible and this makes sense – always providing that getting near the audience does not introduce problems which will more than offset the gain in audience contact. Compromise, as always, is the order of the day: but it must be stressed that the setting line decision is a vitally important one.

FITTING UP

After everything has been hung and flown clear of the stage, the floor is laid. This may be a simple painted stage cloth, but in the design of today's plays it is likely to be a built structure, possibly raked and/or shaped to define an acting 'island' area. The *standing* parts of the set are built next: that is, any pieces which are permanent to the extent of not being moved during performance. The whole set may be standing or just parts of it. The changeable pieces are prepared in the wings and each scene has to be *set and marked*, as the jargon has it: meaning each scene set up and the positions of scenery and furniture marked on the floor. To save time, unless particular difficulties are anticipated, setting and marking can be left until each scene is set during the lighting rehearsal – there is usually quite a lot of time available to consider problems while the lighting cues are plotted. Moreover all the production team are likely to be present and available to agree on any decisions – probably involving compromise – that may be required. Temporary marks are usually made with adhesive tape and more permanent ones with paint. Colour coding can be used to differentiate between scenes. Marks must be as small and as few as is practicable, otherwise they become not only visible to the audience but confusing to the staff. For example, only two of the four legs of chairs and tables need be marked (the usual convention is to mark the upstage pair).

ELECTRICS RIGGING

The bars are by far the quickest part of the electrics rigging operation, but before any bar is flown above stage level it is wise to check it by *flashing out*. Each of the plug tops at the end of the cable-rope or multicore cable feeding the bar is made live in turn, usually by utilising a convenient independent power socket on the side of the stage. At each lamp is checked and proved to be working, its circuit number should be written on the plug top. While this is happening, another electrician should check that all gobos, irises, etc. are fitted, that all colour filters are in, that all profile shutters are fully out, that all barndoors are open, that all safety chains are secure and that all hanging nuts are tight. Once flown, the bar is plugged to the dimmer control system, usually through a permanent socket box on the fly floor. Booms and ladders take more time to rig as they involve spotting special lines from the grid unless (and this rarely happens) the fly rail or an up and downstage flying bar is in precisely the correct position. Booms should be lifted on to a couple of stage weights while their supporting lines are tied off: this ensures that the line is taut when the base is screwed into the stage floor. In most theatres, with the exception of some commercial houses in London and New York, most of the FOH spotlights in the auditorium will be permanent and may need little or no augmentation with extra instruments. They will, however, need colouring and this is an activity that can be usefully slotted in while the stage is occupied by scenery

Flyman's view of a
play with ceiling.

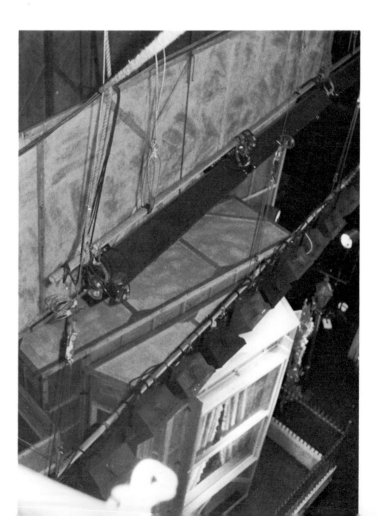

construction. The practice of colouring each light as it is focused is very wasteful of time.

DEADING

The word *dead* has various and confusing meanings in the British theatre. We are here talking about deciding the heights of flown pieces, both scenic and electric. The Americans call this *trim* and avoid confusion. Chapter 5 discusses top and bottom flying deads and also the term *dead line* used to describe a suspension line which is permanently fixed rather than workable from the flys. *Dead it* with reference to a piece of scenery means get rid of it – so *dead scenery* is scenery that has been built for the production but discarded. Keeping scenery *live* on the other hand usually means that the items coming off in a scene change are going to repeat in a later scene and should not be buried at the bottom of the pack. All just a touch confusing!

The deading of the lighting bars and masking borders must be finalised before any of the lighting equipment is focused. In theory the deads, or trims, will have been decided by a study of the section drawing at the planning stage and will now be marked on that drawing. In practice, inspired guesswork is often substituted for accurate calculation and the quality of the inspiration varies. Either way a little flexibility is possible until focusing commences. After this point second thoughts can be rather expensive. The deading is best done by the master carpenter, advised by a committee of scene designer, lighting designer and stage manager. The designer watches from the auditorium while the master carpenter instructs the fly crew from the front row of seating. The lighting designer is mainly interested in checking from the stage that each light will be able to reach its intended target, while the stage manager goes between stage and auditorium, keeping a particular eye on sightlines from the back of the gallery. The checklist of points to be watched (and if necessary compromised between) is design, lighting, masking and sightline. The same process has to be carried out for the side masking, and in both cases it may be necessary to accept inferior masking from front rows and inferior sightline from high back rows because making things perfect for the few might spoil them for the many.

FOCUSING

When rigging of the lights has been completed, the lighting designer should have a quick flash through of all the circuits to check the rig against the plan. Calling the circuit numbers one by one (either in geographical or, possibly better, in numerical sequence) ensures that everything is working and that channel numbers on the control correspond to those on the plan. Wrongly numbered plans are a standard source of time-wasting confusion during the focusing and

Access by tallescope

plotting of lighting: this is the point in the schedule to eliminate that possibility. A flash through at this point will also give some indication of whether each spotlight is likely to be able to do the job assigned to it. For one reason or another, foreseeable or unforeseeable, the light may not be able to hit the desired part of the stage. If this is recognised now, the lighting designer may be able to swop functions between instruments without altering the rig or possibly by swopping colour filters only.

Now comes the laborious job of focusing each light by pointing it at the planned area of stage and adjusting the size, shape and quality of its beam. Access is the main problem and more time is spent in moving and climbing ladders than in actually adjusting lights. In modern theatres, most FOH spotlights are accessible from catwalks: older theatres built before the era of modern lighting require the electrician to be something of a gymnast. On stage it is a matter of ladders. Traditional 'A' ladders have been superseded by a proprietary form of alloy vertical ladder on an adjustable wheeled base, called a *tallescope*, which has become standard in British theatres and has simplified the ladderwork in all departments. Indeed, sharing tallescopes is a vital part of interdepartmental co-ordination as many drama stages are so small that two tallescopes can cause traffic congestion. Focusing requires an electrician up the ladder and a crew to move it around. All ladderwork demands rigid attention to safety procedures, particularly when working on a raked floor. This includes the use of stabilising 'outriggers' on tallescopes plus two crew members holding on to the base. Neglect of these procedures has led to accidents which threaten the introduction of formal bans on the use of some of the most effective access equipment.

In larger theatres, a rigger's control is usually available to light up channels from the stage without the need for anyone in the control room. In smaller theatres, it is often convenient to bring the desk to the stage. Focusing is normally carried out one lamp at a time unless the join between lamps is being checked. When the new number is called, it should be brought on before the previous one is turned off. This saves time and promotes safety by preventing the stage from going to complete blackout. Ideally, the only light on stage will be from the spotlight currently being focused but, in reality, the props and stage crews are likely to be still working and will require some light, although this must of necessity be limited in its brightness and area covered. This is another of these delicate areas of co-ordination and one where split meal times and even split coffee breaks can allow a particular department to have sole occupancy of the stage for a critical task. If the design uses several complete settings, all these will be required in turn for focusing. In more skeletal scenic styles, most of the lights will be focused to the basic set with various scenic elements being flown in or carried on for the focusing of appropriate special lights. If there are many flying pieces, a member of the fly crew should stand by throughout; and a member of the stage management team should always be on call to advise on furniture and actor positions.

PLOTTING THE LIGHTING

After focusing comes the actual 'lighting' – the composition of the lighting pictures as a series of cues for the control board. The director and set designer sit with the lighting designer at the production desk in the auditorium and they should be joined by the member of the stage management team (probably the DSM) who is going to call the cues from the prompt corner. At least one ASM is available to 'walk', that is to take up various actor positions on stage, and the company manager stands by to organise scene changes and to discuss with the team the various technical matters that always crop up at this time. In addition to the plan, the lighting designer has a cue synopsis. The DSM has pencilled these cues into the prompt book. It is useful for the SM to have a copy of the synopsis for checking progress and warning the crew when to stand by for changes.

Scenes are set up exactly and completely, including all furniture and dressings. This will probably be the first time that the director has seen the complete settings on stage and will probably want to experiment with furniture positions while the lighting designer builds the basic lighting picture. This is also the moment to list missing items and jobs to be done. Under lighting, some problems disappear but fresh ones are discovered. Some darkening or texturing of the painting may be necessary in certain areas to take down the harshness from actor lights which unavoidably hit the scenery.

When near to achieving the state of a particular cue, the lighting designer will seek the opinion of the designer and director who may move the ASM(s) about the stage to check actor light in key positions. The lighting designer will have one eye on the clock and as problems arise must decide whether there is time to tackle them now or whether to suggest that they be noted for future action.

When a cue is agreed, the board is asked to plot: the operator must not be hustled but given enough time to plot accurately. With the older pre-memory systems, there was a wait while the level of each channel was written down. This wait provided a useful opportunity for the team to discuss the next cue, but today's plotting is virtually instant. For this reason the cue synopsis has become even more important. However, it is only a guide and should not be adhered to exactly if the business of lighting stimulates some good alternative (and practical) ideas. As soon as plotted, it's on with the next cue. Another bonus of the new controls is that it is now easy and quick to see the effect of the cue change and check its timing.

SOUND EFFECT LEVELS

As the lighting proceeds, the time for the technical rehearsal is fast approaching. Somehow the director has to find time to set sound levels and this probably involves having sandwiches brought to the theatre while everyone else goes out for a more relaxed meal. This is the moment to check the directional placing of the effects loudspeakers and to decide a level for each sound cue.

ACTORS ON STAGE

Actors need time to familiarise themselves with the set. The geography of some designs can be quite complex and even the simplest box setting of a drawing room can spring a few surprises. No matter how well a rehearsal room has been marked out, certain moves, particularly entrances and exits, can only be finally timed on the complete set. Familiarisation may just be individual actors informally trying out their moves or it may need a more formal rehearsal to modify some bit of business that the director, having seen the set, has realised will not quite work. This familiarisation is conveniently carried out in the gap between the end of the lighting rehearsal and the beginning of the tech because the staff need time at this point to take a break before they set up for the beginning of the play.

DRESS PARADE   For a small cast play, a formal dress parade is unlikely to be required. The costume designer will be able to see all the cast individually in the dressing rooms and the director will look them over as they come on stage for rehearsal. For plays with lots of supporting actors, a dress parade becomes another of the events to be squeezed in somewhere – probably just prior to the tech. The state of the costumes at the final fittings will have given some indication of how long the dress parade is likely to take. If the stage schedule is tight, the event can be diverted to somewhere like the stalls bar.

TECHNICAL   There is normally little point in running through a play's technical cues
REHEARSALS   without the cast. If all members of all departments – stage, flys, props, electrics and sound – have properly plotted cue sheets, it is better to try to put it all together with the actors. If time permits, there may be a case for rehearsing scene changes but the crew (with the possible exception of show staff) will have done the changes at least once during the lighting, and possibly twice if there was a separate setting and marking session. It is probably better, therefore, to move on to a full tech and possibly hold a separate session later to polish the trickier moments.

THE TECH   This is sometimes called a stopping dress rehearsal or a stagger-through. The object is to solve every problem as it arises, stopping wherever necessary. The actors give restrained performances, concentrating on moves and 'business' rather on projecting character. This rehearsal is a critical one and it is important to avoid panic. The actors are anxious and the crew are tired. The word 'impossible' may be heard from time to time but it is very important for members of the production team to be able to differentiate between the definitely impossible and the merely difficult. Many good effects have been lost at this point by premature cuts made in panic. On the other hand, when something definitely does not work an alternative must be found – preferably now but certainly before the next rehearsal. How does one decide on difficult versus impossible? Well, remember that although the actors have been at it for weeks, the crew have only just started in the last couple of days or even hours to come to grips with an unfamiliar play and its unfamiliar cue sheets. With a bit of positive thinking one realises how well everyone is doing rather than how badly; how much they are getting right rather than how much they are getting wrong.

The key persons in this stagger-through rehearsal process are the director and stage manager. They must be able to assess the weight that various members of their teams give to words like yes, no, difficult, easy, impossible, try and tomorrow. The role of the stage manager has been discussed in chapter 4 and it must be repeated here that whereas the director may shout 'stop!', the SM must be the one to tell the actors when to start again and where to start from – and will only do this after ascertaining that everyone is ready and set back to the appropriate cue state.

The problem in a stopping rehearsal is to keep some sort of momentum going despite the breaks – success is urging everyone on without alienating them. A knife-edge process! This rehearsal should include the procedure for fading houselights and curtain-up, etc., otherwise the next rehearsal will get off to a bad start. Topping and tailing (cutting dialogue between technical cues) should be avoided unless time shortage makes it absolutely essential. Anyway, unless it is a very simple play, topping and tailing often wastes as much time as it saves due to the time necessary to tell everyone where the restart is and for them to get set up. And the dialogue section that is cut may include the very point where an actor has a door problem.

There should be no need for a note session after the tech. Representatives of all departments will have been watching with the director, discussing and noting problems as they occur. Everyone will have amended their plots and cue sheets and the net result will be that every actor and every technician is exhausted but knows what is supposed to happen.

DRESS REHEARSALS   From this point onwards, the aim is to run without stopping: notes are made of any problems that arise or alterations that are required. Inevitably the rehearsal may come to a grinding halt from time to time, particularly if there are tricky scene changes. For the sake of the actors' concentration, the length of any such stops should be kept to a minimum. Better to pick up the threads as soon as possible, then have an inquest afterwards. Many of the notes arising from the dress rehearsal can be dealt with by discussion but some scenic, prop and lighting matters require exclusive or shared use of the stage. Priorities must be established so that stage time before the next dress rehearsal can be allocated: this will probably include a session for the actors. As the dress rehearsals progress, the number of notes taken is unlikely to get fewer, but they should gradually begin to be about increasingly subtle matters, particularly timing. The point to get worried is when the same notes have to be made at two rehearsals.

PRESS AND PHOTO CALLS

A special call for posed production photographs is now largely a thing of the past. Publicity photographs are taken as action shots during the course of dress rehearsals. The actors should be warned that this is happening and the photographer should be advised about unfinished scenery or costumes. A *press call* has to be slotted into the dress rehearsal schedule: a convenient time for both actors and press is a pre-lunch drinks reception for interviews and photographs. Some of the cast, particularly the younger ladies, may be in costume. (This may seem ageist and sexist, but it is the reality of newspaper interest.) No matter how badly things are going on stage, a pre-arranged press call must be considered as an inviolate arrangement.

FINAL DRESS REHEARSAL

Plays often have only two rehearsals in costume: a tech and a dress. If there is any degree of technical complication in the show it is unfair to have less than three – unfair to the audience as well as author, actors and technicians. Normally the final dress rehearsal is carried through absolutely as performance with the actors trying to cover up mistakes. If the play is a comedy it may be advisable to have a small invited audience to help the actors begin to time the laughs. The final dress rehearsal may have to be during the afternoon of the first performance and there may be difficulty in having a full crew if part-time showmen are being used. However, this is not too disastrous if the scene changes have already been proved to be possible. The final rehearsal belongs to the actors. The production team should be able to take a back seat: if they have done their job properly, it will be virtually over.

PREVIEWS AND FIRST PERFORMANCE

A production may play to an audience before its official opening or *first night* when the press are invited. The preview performances prior to this are not for experiment but to allow the production to mature with the help of audience response. During this period the actors, and often the design team, need the protection of the director from the well-meaning advice offered by a brigade of assorted friends, relatives and agents' wives. A word from the wrong person in the right ear has been known to cause a rewrite of torpedo effect.

It should almost have to go without saying that the production team never, but never, interfere with the running of any performance. No matter what happens, their role is to grit their teeth and make their notes. The stage manager is in total charge once the half-hour has been called.

11   Staging the Musical

The difference between a musical and a play is not so much the music but the scale. There are, of course, exceptions but even a small standing-set musical play such as 'The Fantasticks' uses a company of 15 actors and musicians, a number that is relatively large by the standard of most contemporary plays. There is more to integrate in a musical. There are various groups (principals, chorus and orchestra) indulging in various activities (speaking, singing and dancing) and these group activities have to be rehearsed in every combination. The solitary author becomes a team of workers with individual responsibility for book, lyrics and music. The director becomes the chair of a directing team that includes the choreographer and musical director.

PRIOR TO GET-IN   The technical departments have to prepare *more* of most things: more scenery, more lights, more costumes and more sound. The props department are likely to have less fiddly set dressings but more big props, and while there may be fewer different kinds of hand props, the quantities required may be larger.

The stage management team have a tough job arranging rehearsals. Several adjacent rehearsal rooms are required with intricate scheduling to shuffle actors between the correct dialogue, musical and choreographic sessions. In each type of session actors may work singly, in assorted pairs, trios or ensembles as everything is gradually brought together. Scheduling rehearsal pianists can be one of the trickier aspects of the operation. It is not possible to bring a musical into quite as finalised a rehearsal room state as can be done with a play. A final run-through will show an integration of the acting, singing and dancing in each individual scene but the links between the scenes are likely to be sketchy. This is particularly so in modern musicals where the stage action is continuous and integrated choreographically and musically with the changing scenery.

During the final days in the rehearsal room, the orchestra may have started to rehearse on their own and may have been joined by actors for musical rehearsal. But it is not until the show goes on to the stage with the orchestra in the pit that action can be fully integrated with the orchestrations.

SCHEDULING

It will be appreciated from all this that a musical requires more time between get-in and opening than does a straight play. More time to fit up and more time to rehearse. It is difficult to avoid a lot of overnight work and in the big commercial musicals a combination of various methods is used to make 24-hour progress without causing excessive fatigue.

For a big fit-up in London, freelance crew are hired and/or extra staff borrowed from other theatres. It should be possible to work out some sort of shift system so that everyone gets at least minimum sleep without progress being halted. After the initial basic fit-up is completed, day and night work can be split between departments. Or, probably more productive, the stage can be handed over to the actors for familiarisation rehearsal by day while technical work continues by night. Painters have a lot of touching up to do and painting of the floor is a job often done overnight on site rather than in the studio. And there never was a musical whose stage rehearsals failed to throw up some problems requiring technical alterations of one kind or another.

A musical has to be very simple to be able to get in on Sunday and open on Tuesday or even Wednesday. It can be done and will continue to be done but a successful opening performance under these circumstances relies on an exceptionally experienced technical staff as well as on planning – plus lots of luck and a good measure of adrenalin to produce the magic that pulls a show through by substituting attack for polish.

GETTING IN AND
FITTING UP

There are always exceptions, but generally a musical has more scenery than a play: more volume, more complexity and more changes. Older musicals alternated big full stage scenes with painted front cloths which gave a large staff time to do complete scene changes and a large chorus time to do complete costume changes. Today's musicals aim for continuity by incorporating visible scene changes into the action. They use a permanent decorative surround which gives a stylistic unity to scenic elements dropped in from the flys, trucked on from the sides, or revolved.

To move trucks magically without visible manual assistance but with precision, a big long run musical is set on a specially designed false stage floor. This has track grooves cut into the surface to guide the trucks which are moved by steel wire cables running in the couple of inches of void space between the real stage and the false stage. The trucks are usually moved by hand-operated winches although motors are some-

"MAN OF LA MANCHA" – PICCADILLY THEATRE

STAGE	ELECTRICS

SATURDAY MARCH 30th
The following work should be completed by 1.00 p.m.
1. Covering of House Velvet with black moilé (Mr. Tomlin)
2. Measuring up preparations and deliveries of material for: (a) Fencing around stage
   (b) Filling in stage behind cyc sweeps
   (c) Sound deadening partition frame (Harry Pegg and Babbages)
3. Contractors complete demolition leaving site clear and basement floor swept clean for painting. (Sinclairs & H. Pegg)
4. Delivery of lifting bridge, hanging quatrefoil frame, d.s. wing frames, tunnel. (Babbages)
 	
4.00 p.m.
Two men to paint central basement area black.
THIS MUST BE DRY BY : 9.00 a.m.
	1. Installation of horn speakers over & at sides of pros. (S. Coppin and C.K. Electronics).
	2. Installation and testing of cwt 8 hoist.

SUNDAY MARCH 31st
7.00 a.m. Babbages   : 2 men
           H. Pegg   }
           H. Robinson} + 6 men
Hang cyc and leave doubled up in grid. Hang quatrefoil frame
Fit-up d.s. wing frames
Assemble lifting bridge & leave on basement floor.
Fill-in stage behind cyc sweeps
Fence side stages & prepare run of fences across rear stage
	NO CALL FOR ELECTRICS

MONDAY APRIL 1st 9.00 a.m. 1. Fly bridge on motorised cwt 8 and chain tackle (Balls) (leave at good working height for scenic artist) Complete fixings and brackets for rear platform bridge 10.00 a.m. 1. Scaffolding dismantle and get-out FOH scaffolding (Clarke & Fenn + Modern Scaffolding). 2. Geoffrey Guy to paint lifting bridge & quatrefoil frame (at basement level) 3. Mark out & prepare for arrival of main set (H. Pegg) 4. When Geoffrey Guy finished, lift flying pieces clear of basement and swing of scene dock hoist.	Work with Balls as necessary, etc. Check all speakers and box booms rigged & OK before scaffolding dismantled.
TUESDAY APRIL 2nd 7.00 a.m. Dismantle scaffolding at REHEARSAL THEATRE and get-out by 10.30 a.m. (use entrance staircase) (Tasker & Booth) 9.30 a.m. – REHEARSAL THEATRE – H. Robinson) + 12 men Babbages – 2 men until 11 pm Start dismantling set from front to back and get-out 11.00 a.m. 2 Coales lorries ready for loading at (main dock doors). Shuttle service to Piccadilly (on first lorry 6 men travel to unload & start get-in). When set assembled Babbages 2 men go to Piccadilly & start re-assembly with: H. Pegg } + 8 men (reducing to approx 4 to 5 men H. Robinson } from 6.00 to 11.00 p.m.) 1.00 p.m. Additional two carpenters from Babbages to work through evening and night until fit-up completed Wednesday morning 11.00 Rehearsal Theatre : H. Robinson + 7 men get-out remainder of set on to 1 Coales lorry (shuttle service to Piccadilly) Piccadilly : H. Pegg + 1 man continue working with Babbages carpenters, joined by H. Robinson + 7 men with last load. ALL WORK THROUGH NIGHT UNTIL FIT-UP COMPLETED & PARTITION BUILT BEHIND CYC	Remove dustsheets from booms and ladders. Fit new FOH wall brackets.

STAGE	ELECTRICS
WEDNESDAY APRIL 3rd 8.00 a.m. Fit-up rear platform bridge (Ball's) 9.00 a.m. Hetherington's start laying felt and rubber flooring and making good fibre-glass joints (work all night, if necessary, to complete by Thursday lunch-time) Stage staff break when fit-up completed, and after checking that Ball's and Hetherington's require no assistance. 2.00 p.m. Scenic artists (G. Guy) start painting main set (work all night)	Remove dust-sheets from spot bars. Set-up and check intercom systems, cue lights, blue lights, etc, and sound effects system. Complete preparations for focussing. Provide good work-light overnight for scenic artists.
THURSDAY APRIL 4th 9.00 a.m. Ball's & Harry Pegg } + 6 men Harry Robinson } Lower cyc and cut hole, and lower quatrefoil frame, as necessary, to allow lifting bridge to hinge on to fixed platform bridge. Test lifting bridge mechanically. 3.00 p.m. NB: At least one skilled flyman should be on duty on counter-weight system while focussing is in progress from cradles with a second responsible person at stage level.	Test lifting bridge electrically. Focussing until last transport
FRIDAY 5th APRIL 9.00 a.m. Set up props etc (Stage Management) Fit new orchestra posts & chains (Ball's) 7.30 a.m. ARTISTS REHEARSE ON STAGE	Continue focussing until finished. WORKING LIGHT ONLY
SATURDAY 6th APRIL 9.00 a.m. 10.00 a.m.	Prepare for lighting Plot lighting through until last transport
SUNDAY 7th APRIL ARTISTS REHEARSE ON STAGE ALL DAY	WORKING LIGHT ONLY
MONDAY 8th APRIL 9.00 a.m. Prepare for Technical Rehearsal 2.00 p.m. FIRST TECHNICAL REHEARSAL WITH LIGHTING (TO FINISH BEFORE LAST TRANSPORT, EVEN IF ONLY PARTIALLY COMPLETED)	Complete plotting
TUESDAY 9th APRIL Morning: Technical work on stage Stretch cyc properly and lay floor panels. Afternoon: ARTISTS REHEARSE ON STAGE 6.00 p.m. TECHNICAL REHEARSAL (EITHER PICK UP FROM WHERE STOPPED PREVIOUS NIGHT, OR BEGIN AGAIN FROM TOP)	Technical work on stage WORKING LIGHT ONLY
WEDNESDAY 10th APRIL Morning: Technical work on stage Afternoon: ARTISTS REHEARSE ON STAGE 6.00 p.m. : FIRST DRESS REHEARSAL (FULL – EX ORCHESTRA?)	Technical work WORKING LIGHT ONLY

Detailed schedule for the get-in of 'Man of La Mancha'. The full schedule included the countdown (rerouting of services, etc.) prior to the conclusion of the previous production so that the stage floor could be removed to allow the setting to be built up from the basement floor. After the run of 'Man of La Mancha', the Piccadilly Theatre was equipped with a removable modular stage floor.

times used. Any such false floor is usually laid as the first operation of the fit-up: this means that it has to be the first item to be unloaded and into the theatre. If dock space is tight, it may be necessary to lay the floor before unloading anything else. Next step, as in a play, is the hanging although this is likely to be much more complex with lots of French flats to be built. The number of hangings in a musical is often greater than the number of lines available. Whether the extra lines are

Stage plan for one of the many scenes in a fast moving musical production.

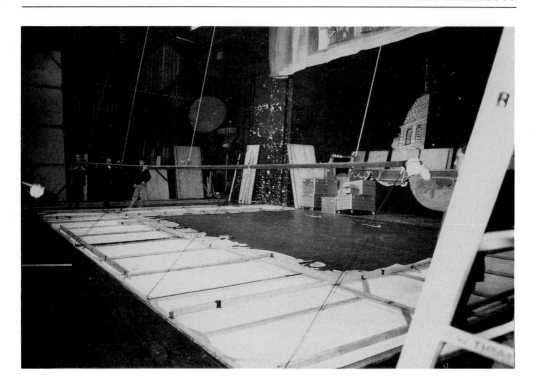

One of the portals of a permanent decorative surround assembled on the stage floor, with wires attached in readiness for flying.

installed with motors, temporary counterweights, or just hemp will depend on weight to be flown and length of run. The flown scenery is then so tightly packed that breasting lines may have to be run across from one fly gallery to the other to make space for a flown piece to move on cue by easing adjacent non-moving pieces upstage or downstage out of the way. Hanging must be completed before the masking surround is built, because a full clear stage area is required for laying down and battening out the French flats. There is often decorative masking consisting of a series of portals, each formed from a pair of wing flats joined by a framed border. The downstage portal is called the false proscenium, shortened to *false pros.*

Basically the fit-up processes outlined for plays in the last chapter are applicable to musicals. The main differences are scale and time, and the effect of this on interdepartmental co-ordination has been discussed under scheduling. Some other points of difference to be considered are . . .

LIGHTING

There is a lot of lighting to focus: much of it is general, some is specific to particular scenes. The best procedure is probably to move through the rig in sequence, focusing as much as possible on a stage empty except for

The portal being slowly raised to hang vertically.

permanent masking but with a flyman standing by to drop in flown pieces as required. Spotlights which can only be focused to a built scene should be passed over or perhaps just roughly set. After the general focusing session has been completed, scenes which have several special spotlights can be built for focusing. If a scene is complicated to build and/or only has one or two specials, it may be more economic to leave the focusing of these until the scene is set during the plotting session. Side lighting from booms and ladders tends to be general as does much of the FOH: so it is sensible to start with one of these, remembering that it is easier to shout instructions to the FOH when the theatre is quiet, perhaps during a split meal break or during the night. The lighting rehearsal, in addition to plotting light cues, is the time to clarify the co-ordination of scenery and lighting movements in the scene changes. Even after detailed planning, the most effective way of doing such moves often does not become obvious until this point (but planning is still required: it is easier to alter a plan than to have no plan at all).

Limes

Musicals usually have follow spots: at least two, often four and occasionally more. Both the follow spot and its operator are frequently referred to as *limes* although it is a long time since the light source was a

Backstage at a musical.

piece of lime made incandescent in an oxy-hydrogen jet. Most follow spots now use discharge lamps but low voltage beamlights have become increasingly popular for short throws. Ideally the lime operators should watch a run-through, preferably with the lighting designer, to get an overall familiarity with the show. Alternatively, the principals should be brought in front of the curtain to be introduced to the limes before the first tech.

TECHNICAL REHEARSALS

Musicals inevitably involve the use of part-time crew, therefore full scale technical and dress rehearsing may only be practicable in the evening. Day rehearsals can solve the technical problems of working on individual scenes: entrances, exits, use of levels, spacing of choreography, etc. There are a lot of matters that can be be cleaned up by actors, choreographer and director in each set. The lighting designer can start to check the balance of cues against the actor positions and the sound designer can start to prepare cues, although it will be too early to start sound balancing as not only will there be no orchestra but the actors will not be singing out.

If problems within scenes are worked on in this way, the evening technical stagger-throughs can be devoted to problems which concern everyone: the links to get out of one scene and into the next. To do the job properly on a musical needs at least two evenings: Act I tonight and Act II tomorrow. And on the big shows this may become at least two full days. This allows technical problems to be sorted out before the orchestra joins to add a whole new series of musical problems.

MUSICAL REHEARSALS

The first *band calls* held in a rehearsal room, often the theatre bar, are to sort out the notes. Singers join later band calls as a check on the correctness of the accompaniments and to familiarise themselves with the orchestrations. But it is only once the orchestra is in the pit that balance between voice and instruments can be worked out, including foldback levels for the singers to hear not just the orchestra but their own voices. Also, it is only at this point that choreographer and conductor can finalise the dance tempi, and the dancers be given a chance to synchronise with the totally different sound of the orchestra compared with a rehearsal piano. Most of this can be done either without scenery, or with essential bits such as levels built in skeleton form only. During such a rehearsal, the sound plot begins to take shape and the sound operator should be given some idea of the extent to which individual singers are saving their voices rather than singing out.

**DRESS
REHEARSALS**

Orchestra time is very expensive and overtime is paid for in sacks of gold. It makes sense, therefore, to have done two things thoroughly before a full dress rehearsal: first, to have rehearsed the whole show technically with piano and, secondly, to have rehearsed individual scenes on stage with orchestra. To rush into a full orchestral dress rehearsal without this groundwork is likely to result in expensive, depressing chaos. But with the suggested preparation, the first dress rehearsal should hold together with scene changes as the only really tricky moments. That there may be too much or too little scene change music may not be discovered until this point because a rehearsal pianist can 'vamp till ready' more easily than can a full orchestra. To get through a full dress rehearsal without the show falling apart is a splendid morale boost to everyone – but especially to the actors who can now concentrate on matters like characterisation and pace, rather than the struggle to master technicalities which has been their concern since leaving the rehearsal room.

**MUSICAL
HYSTERIA**

It would be unrealistic to fail to mention at this time that the big musicals are very rarely staged in an atmosphere of calm. They stretch available resources and they stretch people, requiring detailed co-ordination between a bunch of individualists. And they represent a big financial investment. Everyone has a cure for the show's problems, whether they be real or imaginary, and often the best bits of the show are the ones that get cut. It is a rare commercial musical that reaches curtain up on the opening night without someone walking out or getting fired. There is no magical recipe for avoiding the contagious panic that causes all this – but good planning and communications help to create a sense of purpose and a feeling that progress is being made. And these are the major requirements for creating a happy company.

12　Staging Opera

Our discussion of plays and musicals has assumed that they were being staged for a 'run' – that they had sole occupancy of the stage for the period covering their staging rehearsals and performances, that is, sole occupancy from get-in to get-out. Most plays and musicals, at least in Anglo-American theatre practice, are mounted in this way but in turning our attention to *opera* we are looking at a stage form which is almost always played in *repertoire*, or that variation of repertoire known as *stagione* and already discussed in chapter 2. Opera is performed in repertoire mainly to conserve the singer's voices: the strain of sustaining a big role every night will wreck a voice, particularly in its formative years. Also a repertoire programme suits the opera audience who like to see favourite established operas on a repeating basis, whereas most playgoers thrive on a diet of new drama. (Again we are speaking mainly of Anglo-American theatre. The situation is rather different in Central Europe where drama is also played largely in repertoire and with a strong classical bias.)

Some of the problems discussed in this chapter are special to opera, but many of them are general repertoire problems arising out of the special circumstances of performing and rehearsing several productions concurrently, whether they be operatic, balletic or dramatic.

OPERA COMPANIES

There are two kinds of opera companies: *permanent* and *ad hoc*. The permanent companies perform in their own theatres with full-time orchestra, chorus and technicians. They have a nucleus of singers under annual contract but rely heavily for leads upon a pool of freelance singers – national or international depending on the status of the company. Ad hoc companies are formed for short seasons or for special performances at festivals. Even if an ad hoc company is only performing one opera, it generally has to be organised on repertoire lines as the stage is likely to be used by other performances during the season.

REHEARSALS

Opera rehearsals are two-part: musical and production. Before the first production rehearsals, the singers study their roles individually with a

REHEARSAL SCHEDULE - SUNDAY MAY 29th

STAGE:	5.30 for 5.40	DON GIOVANNI F.R.
REHEARSAL STAGE:	10.30-1.30) 10pm - 12 midnight)	FALSTAFF Production Rehearsal
HECTOR:	10.30-1.30	DON GIOVANNI Production Rehearsal (Understudies)
	3.00-5.00	VIXEN Production Rehearsal

DON GIOVANNI F.R.

5.30 for 5.40	ACT I: Dean, Luxon, Carden, Andrade, Goeke, Thau, Rawnsley, Gale, FULL CHORUS, Supers	PRITCHARD HALL MALLANDAINE CLEOBURY WILDER PETER-SZABO
7.10 approx.	LONG INTERVAL	
8.25 for 8.35	ACT II CAST as above, MENS CHORUS, Supers, Richards.	

ALL PRINCIPALS IN DRESSING ROOMS 1 HOUR BEFORE FIRST APPEARANCE PLEASE

1.30-9.45pm　　GREEN ROOM RESERVED AS A QUIET REST ROOM

Warm-ups			
11.00	Carden	PETER-SZABO	Louise
4.15	Luxon	MALLANDAINE	Rehearsal Stage
4.45	Andrade	"	
5.10	Gale	"	

Production Rehearsal Understudies

10.30	Plowright, Rath, M. Lewis	Hector
11.30	Plowright, Rath, K. Lewis, Harrhy	TROTTER
12.30	Plowright, Harrhy, K. Lewis, M. Lewis, Rath	FRASER
1.00	Price joins	

VIXEN:　　　　3.00-5.00　Production Rehearsal

3.00	Cannan, Flowers, M-Bruce, Korman, Herford	Hector
4.30	McKinnon joins	VICK WARD FRASER

Musical Rehearsals

10.30-12.00	Herford	WARD
12.15-1.30	Nemeer	WARD

FALSTAFF:

10.30-1.30) 10pm-12midnight)	Production Rehearsal	Ptolemy Ptolemy
11.30-1.30	I/1 Capecchi, (Kerry), Trama Dickerson, Nemeer, Fryatt, Page-boy	Rehearsal Stage PONNELLE eve HOPE (PRITCHARD)
10p.m.-12 midnight Capecchi, Ellis		BRADSHAW WILDER a.m. MALLANDAINE eve

SCHWEIGSAME FRAU

10.30-1.30) 2.30-5.30)	Ensemble	Organ Room DAVIS, HINDEN
10.30	Peters, Gottlieb, Cross	BRAITHWAITE
11.00-1.30) 2.30-5.30)	Cast by arrangement after Saturday evening rehearsal.	(FIFIELD) BEALa.m. BARLON a.m. (WILDER)
2.30-3.30	Peters	BEAL, BARLOW
3.45-5.00	Summerscales	BEAL
	Cannan	BARLON Conductor's Room Conductor's Room Ptolemy

CHORUS:

4.55	DON GIOVANNI FULL CHORUS Warm-up Lily Davis Room	
5.30 for 5.40	DON GIOVANNI F.R.	

N.A.:　　Brodie, Bowman, Davia

CATERING　The Staff Restaurant will be open 12.30-2.00 & Long Interval - NO GUESTS PLEASE

MAY　　　　　　Week: 7

		THURSDAY 26	FRIDAY 27	SATURDAY 28	SUNDAY 29
THEATRE 1	M	10.30-1.30 Vixen w.o.			
	A	2.30-4p.m. Vixen w.o. 4.15-5.30 Voix o.a.	2.00-5p.m. 2 x Don w.o./C/Light	2.00-5p.m. 1 x Vixen wo/C Lights	
	E	Tech	6-9p.m.	6.30-7.15p.m. Voix Sitz w.o. 7.30-9.30p.m. Voix w.o.	5.30 DON FINAL REH.
REHEARSAL STAGE 2	M	2 x Falstaff w.p.	2 x Falstaff w.p.	2 x Falstaff w.p.	2 x Falstaff w.p.
	A				
	E				
PRODUCTION 3	M	1 x Don underst. w.p.	1 x Vixen underst. w.p.	1 x Don underst. w.p.	1 x Don underst. w.p.
	T				1 x Vixen underst. w.p.
	E				
MUSIC 4	M			S. Frau mus.	S. Frau mus.
	A			W. Davis	W. Davis
	E				
N.A. 5		Peters Lott	Braithwaite Fr. 5pm Allen Matheson-Bruce fr 5pm Cannan	Braithwaite Plowright Peters Matheson-Bruce Gottlieb J.	
ARRIVE 6				Davis	
DEPART 7			Stage II pm eve Phillips eve eve	Isepp (to June 13)	Fraser
NOTES 8		Matheson-Bruce on recall ENO		Matheson-Bruce on recall ENO	

The weekly schedule for the summer opera festival at Glyndebourne is circulated several months before the first rehearsals. Updating amendments follow regularly and a daily schedule is issued each afternoon with a detailed breakdown for the next day.

repetiteur (a pianist-coach, probably with conducting ambitions). There are also ensemble musical rehearsals and so every member of the cast comes to the first production rehearsal knowing their part. As a result, production rehearsals can be more concentrated than those for a play or musical. Fewer sessions are required than with other forms of theatre, but because the singers are performing during the evenings – in the same opera house or elsewhere – the rehearsals tend to be spread over a longer period. This spreading of rehearsals applies to the technical and dress rehearsals as well as to the earlier rehearsal rooom sessions. Because of daily performances, the pattern of use of the stage tends to be morning rehearsal, afternoon preparation for performance, then the evening performance. For preparation of a particularly heavy rehearsal or performance, overnight working can be added. Most round-the-year opera houses have two technical crews working a shift system, sometimes overlapping at the heaviest part of the day, the afternoon changeover from rehearsal to performance. Since the stage is only available for rehearsals in the mornings, the staging period is spread over something like a fortnight. There are advantages in that some of the pressure is removed and time is available between rehearsals for a re-think of any problems that have appeared. On the other hand, big disadvantages stem from the requirement that the whole technology of the production must be geared to quick setting and striking on a twice daily basis.

SCHEDULES

There is an extra element in opera scheduling, always referred to as 'N/As', meaning non-availabilities. Singers may not be able to rehearse on certain days because they are resting before a particularly strenuous evening performance. Or freelances may be performing or rehearsing elsewhere. Small part singers may be rehearsing for two productions at the same time: it is common for an opera house to have one production in dress rehearsal while the next one is in the rehearsal room. And the chorus may be N/A on a particular day to avoid incurring overtime payments. Wherever possible N/As are agreed at the time of signing contracts, but to foster good relations with popular singers, managements often grant extra N/As at short notice. It is therefore not unknown for important rehearsals to include understudies or 'covers' as they are more generally known in the opera world.

Long term schedules block out the allocation of stage, pit and the various rehearsal rooms on a sessional basis. To ease planning of alterations, this schedule should contain an N/A column. Additionally, detailed schedules are published weekly and/or daily with a breakdown of each rehearsal and performance into the times at which various performers and personnel are called.

REHEARSAL ROOMS

Opera production rehearsal rooms have to be large – at least as large as the full stage acting area – because of the large numbers of cast, the large gestures that they make, and the large volumes of sound that they produce. There is also a large production team to be accommodated: director, conductor, choreographer, chorus master, coaches and stage management. And they all have assistants. Because of the nature of operatic scenery and the intensive rehearsal programme, it is desirable that at least the various scenic levels can be provided for rehearsals. Special rehearsal rooms are often built to make this possible: at Glyndebourne, for example, there is a rehearsal stage on the same level as the main stage so that trucked scenery can be moved easily between the two.

FITTING UP

A new production generally gets on to the stage about ten or more days before the first performance. The ideal day is a *production Sunday* or whatever day of the week is a particular opera house's closed day (closure on both Sunday and Monday simplifies the whole operation). As the scenery is constructed for rapid daily setting and striking, it should go up relatively easily, even at first attempt. Opera stage facilities vary a great deal. Some have enough space adjacent to the stage to permit all trucks to be kept built for the current repertoire; others have to break down the trucks daily and some even have to get operas out daily for transport to distant storage. The big German-inspired stages of Central Europe have full-size side and rear rolling stages, so that complete sets can be driven on to the main stage acting area. These may be used for a single opera but, particularly in smaller cities, it is more common to use them to shift around the various complete operas between rehearsal and performance. The availability of rehearsal stages certainly simplifies fitting up, since parts of the scenes are likely to have been built already for rehearsal and construction snags discovered.

LIGHTING

There are two methods of dealing with lighting in a repertoire theatre. Both are based on a permanent rig, for there is no time to hang any but the very minimum essential extra bars or booms. One system, particularly favoured by Central European theatres in the German tradition, uses a relatively small number of spotlights mounted on access bridges, towers and galleries. These are manned by a large permanent trained lighting staff who re-focus and angle some of the lights in scene changes and also follow the singers with others. When the repertoire is large, there may be a couple of weeks between performances of a particular work and it can be difficult for singers to be absolutely precise in taking up stage positions. Also, substitute singers may have to go on with limited rehearsal. All this is easier to cope with when the lights are manned. German opera houses have an adjustable false proscenium which carries horizontal bridges and vertical towers. These bridges and towers move with the proscenium when it is adjusted to give the appropriate height and width to frame a scene. Grids are much higher so that borders are rarely needed for masking and are only introduced if required for decoration. This means that a three-tier lighting bridge can reach all positions upstage while maintaining a reasonable lighting angle.

(*left*) Backstage in one of the smaller German opera houses. The lighting equipment is mounted on a bridge and tower structure so that it is accessible for focusing between, or even during, scenes. The bridge and towers form a false proscenium which is adjustable to the size required for a particular production.

The alternative system is a saturation rig which, as its name implies, rams the maximum number of spotlights possible into the theatre, both FOH and backstage. These spots are classified in three ways: (1) permanently focused for a systematic general coverage, (2) focused as specials for particular productions and locked-off in these positions, and (3) re-focused daily as required. Until recently, the selection required to meet the needs of a particular production was made at a patch panel or by cross-plugging at the socket boxes feeding the various lighting positions. However, the latest control systems make the selection by a soft patching program in the computer software.

Where the theatre architecture permits an on-stage bridge and towers, there is a lot to be said in favour of a compromise system using a reasonably large number of lights with a small attendant staff. Certainly the standard procedures of the straight play are no use – there is no time to set up Act II Sc 4 in the afternoon just to focus a couple of spotlights. Yet this scene may arrive in a 40-second musical scene change. No time for ladders! And the set only needs to be slightly off its marks for a spotlight shuttered into a window to make a nasty splodge: a moment when there is no real substitute for an electrician on a bridge.

Some opera companies lay numbered canvas strips on the stage floor, at right angles to one another along the centre and setting lines. These act as co-ordinates for a grid system of plotting light beam positions on an empty stage. During changeovers this allows the spotlights to be focused quickly before the scenery is built, because a tallescope ladder can be wheeled easily to all parts of the empty stage. The system works well for general coverage, but precision shutterings have to be checked after the scenery is set.

It should be emphasised that the procedures of lighting preparation and rehearsal are exactly the same as those described for play and musical except for the disciplines imposed by consideration of, and respect for, the needs of other works in the repertoire.

| STAGE MANAGEMENT | The prompt book in an opera house is an interleaved copy of the vocal score with the cues marked to be given on specific notes in specific bars. Opera stage management have to know enough about musical notation to be able to prepare and read this kind of prompt copy. It is just not possible to take cues from words or actions. In opera, the timing is controlled by the conductor and not by the actors: in most cases the music cannot wait for a missed cue in the way that actors can ad lib or vary the pace so that a late scenic movement can catch up. Opera cues are therefore given precisely with the music, watching the stage only to check safety and perhaps to integrate the type of cue sequence where a cloth must be dropped in before the lights are brought up. It is customary in opera for a member of the stage management staff (but not the one in the corner, running the show) to check that singers are ready for entrances and sometimes to cue them on. Backstage, in addition to normal stage management cueing, there is likely to be at least one member of the music staff to conduct off-stage choruses, bands, drum rolls, fanfares, etc. |

Prompting is also a province of the music staff rather than the stage management. Because the orchestral accompaniment continues when a singer forgets a line, prompting after the event is too late. Prompting has to be in advance and, as it is difficult to tell just when a singer is going to dry, every line has to be hissed out by the prompter from a little box in the centre of the footlights. As opera becomes regarded more and more as musical theatre, the services of a prompter tend to be considered unnecessary. However, an opera house always needs prompt box facilities to use in emergencies such as sudden cast replacements due to illness.

PIANO DRESS REHEARSAL	The key staging rehearsal, equivalent to the tech in a playhouse, is the piano dress. Hopefully, individual scenes will already have been tackled on stage with scenery and props. Now the whole opera is put together: singers, costumes, props, lights, effects, etc. The only missing element is the orchestra. The piano dress is the final production rehearsal to belong exclusively to the director. The singers concentrate on production problems and only occasionally open out vocally. Although music takes a back seat, it is to be hoped that the conductor will take part rather than send a deputy. An opera conductor has rather more to do than in the concert hall: there is a lot of integration required between pit and production, particularly on exits and entrances, and at the beginnings and ends of scenes. The piano dress is the time to get all this straight, for this is the last rehearsal at which it will be possible to stop and go back for anything other than musical problems. Opera rehearsals are generally in three-hour sessions and a piano dress will normally be allocated two such sessions to allow time for stopping to clear up problems. As always at this point in rehearsals, it is the stage manager who must get the rehearsal re-started after a stop: in this case by cueing the conductor.

SITZPROBE

After the orchestra have had their own rehearsals, they meet up with the singers at a session called the *sitzprobe*. This is a purely musical rehearsal with, traditionally, a row of chairs set out at the front of the stage for the singers. Sometimes, particularly in theatres with an inclination to view opera rather more as music theatre, this rehearsal takes the form of a 'walking sitzprobe' where singers move about to take up their appropriate stage positions. The stage management find the sitzprobe useful for getting accustomed to following the prompt score while listening to the orchestral sound after weeks of rehearsal piano.

ORCHESTRAL DRESS REHEARSALS

As indicated earlier, dress rehearsals are to be regarded primarily as musical rehearsals. It is the role of the director and technical staff to keep quiet and make notes unless real problems occur and they are forced or asked to intervene. The stage manager will only halt the rehearsal in the event of danger or a really major technical problem. However, the conductor may stop for musical reasons. Some of these stops will be made for off-stage music: there is nothing quite like a distant trumpet call for bringing an entire opera house to a grinding halt. Other stops will be about difficulties in seeing the conductor, and the director may have to rearrange moves and positions. Whether to amend or whether to hold out for a further attempt to make the original ideas work requires a fine degree of judgement of how real the problem is. Moments like this soon show up how well the director and conductor have worked together on a joint concept.

After these dress rehearsals, two types of note sesssion may be required: production and musical. Any time remaining before the end of the three-hour orchestral session is used to go back over balance or ensemble problems. Individual vocal problems are usually dealt with in special coaching sessions. Director's notes usually have to be given in a rehearsal room to make the stage available for changeover to the evening performance.

GENERAL REHEARSAL

The final rehearsal before the opening performance is called the *general* and is sometimes played, rather in the nature of a preview, to an invited audience. Rehearsals for a new production place quite a strain on voices and it is customary to have the general 48 hours before the opening night to allow a full day's rest in between.

REVIVALS

Much of the foregoing discussion has been about the introduction of new productions into the repertoire. This may be the more exciting part of the work but the standing of an opera house and its obligation to its audience depend upon maintaining the standard of productions for as long as they remain in the repertoire and on their subsequent revival. The staging standards of a production are kept up to scratch by a staff director who was probably assistant director during the original mounting of the opera. This staff director watches all performances and rehearses any cast changes, then acts as director when the opera is revived in future seasons, if the original diretctor is not available or is unwilling to rehearse the revival in person.

Plans and plots of all kinds must be particularly detailed as operas which have been out of the repertoire for a considerable time, even years, tend to get revived with minimum technical rehearsal. Photographic records are particularly useful checks of scenery and prop settings, and some opera houses file *progress shot* photographs showing move-by-move sequences of singer groupings.

TEMPERAMENT

It is popularly thought that opera singers are very temperamental. Not true – the reverse is the case. Opera singers have to continue to study and practise their techniques throughout their careers and, in the author's experience, often demonstrate a far more professional approach to their work than many performers in other branches of theatre.

13   Staging the Dance

It is logical to consider ballet immediately after opera since they both perform in repertoire and they often share the same stage. An opera house can supply two basic needs of ballet: a big stage and a big orchestra. Or at least these were the basic requirements until the development of modern dance companies playing in any kind of performance space from the large formal proscenium stage to the informal studio area, and preferring tape or chamber ensemble to the traditional full orchestra. However, whatever the scale, there are certain problems common to all modes of dance staging.

SCENERY   Much of the dance repertoire comprises short single-act works and it is even quite common for programmes to include single acts selected from the relatively small number of full-length classical ballets. There can be quite a lot of interval in a dance evening: four acts with three intervals is not uncommon and these intervals have to be longish to allow the dancers to recover and do a complete costume and possibly make-up change. This means that there is not usually a time problem with interval scene changes. Many one-act ballets have no changes within the act and where there is a change it is often just a simple fly cue (although there are, as always, exceptions – 'Petrushka', for example, depends on slick major changes). So the main scenic problems are those associated with the daily round of rehearsal and performance. This is further complicated because an evening's programme may be made up from various combinations of the available one-act repertoire. Two short works which have always seemed simple may suddenly become a problem when played together on the same evening. However, most dance scenery is technically straightforward. The dancers basically require a flat stage area so there is a distinct lack of the rostra and steps to give the levels that other theatre forms demand. The standard format is backcloth and wings, and many short pieces use only a backcloth and plain black wings. The big classics make full use of backcloths, gauzes and limited built scenery. The quality of the stage floor is very important, both in smoothness and springiness. Special vinyl floor coverings are standard. These are rolled for touring and the joints taped when laid.

LIGHTING   Most ballets require a good overall coverage in a choice of colour washes with lots of side lighting to sculpture the dancer's bodies and emphasise the dimensional quality of their limb movements. This is generally supplied by a spot bar upstage of each border for top light and high side light, with a tower upstage of each wing for low side light. Towers are generally preferred to conventional booms or ladders as they can be moved upstage or downstage in act changes to adjust to the varying positions of wing flats. The towers consist of a heavily weighted wheeled base supporting a vertical boom of about 12 or 14 ft (3.5–4 m) in height.

Portable towers are used for side lighting dancers.

The resultant light is close to horizontal and this is a good angle for limb lighting. To avoid shadows being cast on the wings at the opposite side of the stage, the wings are angled so that the onstage edge is very slightly downstage. From the front, the wing looks parallel to the front of the stage but the slight angle stops it from receiving shadows.

It is difficult to colour hanging equipment during an interval change but it can and has been done. Most companies, however, try to fit colour scrollers to a proportion of their overhead lights and keep static filters in the rest. Filters can be changed for each act in the more accessible side lighting. Because the emphasis is on body movement rather than facial expression, dance tends to use less FOH lighting than other forms of theatre.

Follow spots are sometimes used to emphasise the soloists, particularly in classical ballet, but a single conventional follow spot can flatten a dancer's sculptural movements. If follow spots are used, there should be at least two, possibly three, from angles appropriate to dimensional sculpturing.

Some modern choreography has sequences which do not use the whole stage but involve almost stationary dancers using only subtle movements. For this, selective area lighting is appropriate and such works tend to have many more cues than the more open full-stage style of ballets.

ORGANISATION Staging organisation is not unlike that of an opera company. Ballet companies resident in opera houses generally share the opera's technical facilities and most of its staff except stage management. Dancers have the most extensive schedule of all performing artists, including daily class as well as rehearsals and performances. This needs detailed planning, and when rehearsal rooms are not available on tour the technical work of the stage has to be organised to leave the stage free for rehearsal during as much of the day as possible, even if this involves overnight technical work. Fortunately many of the settings are so simple that comparatively little time is required for daily changeover.

14 Staging Light Entertainment

The expression *light entertainment* is not intended to imply that the forms of theatre discussed in previous chapters are heavy and serious. Nor is this chapter about light shows, colour music, son et lumière or any other types of entertainment dependent on fluid light rather than actors. Light entertainment is a useful television classification for a group of types of show for which there is no collective theatre term. The group includes revue, variety, pantomimes, and to put it rather basically, any forms of show that are put together with scissors and paste. The basis of such shows is that varying amounts of the performance material (script, music, props, costumes, etc.) are supplied by the performers themselves in a ready-made rehearsed form. A light entertainment performance is compiled rather than written and consists of a series of *acts* joined together by *production.* The proportion of specially written material included with the acts and the degree to which the acts are integrated into the production varies according to the type of show.

VARIETY (VAUDEVILLE)

A true variety bill is a series of self-contained acts without any linking material between them. After the applause at the end of one act, the orchestra go straight into the music of the next act. This immediate musical join is called a *segue* and the term is used a lot in theatre jargon (usually emphasised as *dead segue*) to describe any immediate follow on. Variety bills are only occasionally performed in theatres nowadays. Variety has completed a full cycle from pub through music hall and variety theatre to club where its acts play to an audience once again seated at refreshment tables.

Variety acts are complete mini-productions. They have their own scripts, music, costumes and props (variety actors usually call themselves *artistes* and they use the word 'props' to cover both props and wardrobe). The only item that they do not carry is scenery, relying on the resident stage manager to provide a suitable background. Among the sadly disappearing traditional arts and crafts of the theatre is the ingenuity with which the resident stage managers decorated their stages week after week with every conceivable combination and permutation of stock drapes. Artists normally structure their acts so that the closing section can be performed downstage to allow the indispensable tabs ('No 1 runners') to be closed behind them to enable the next act to set their props.

Variety artists write their lighting plots (traditionally, on the backs of box-office advertising cards) in terms of the colour washes produced by red, blue and white battens and floats, with limes assumed to be in use unless specified otherwise. The possibilities are:

Full up	Blackout
Red Stage	Pin focus
Blue Stage	FUF
Colours	Iris out

Most of these are obvious. 'Pin focus', often asked for with a blackout, means a tight lime (head only). There are two ways of ending a musical number. 'FUF' (full-up-finish) meaning build up to full over the last bar(s) of music to get applause, and 'iris out' meaning slowly fade everything towards the end of the number with the lime irising smaller and smaller and finally out on the last note – count 2, 3 and UP full for applause. No

A typical lighting plot for a variety act.

BILLY CROCKETT'S 2ND SPOT

TRUMPET	COLOURS + FUF
SMALL SAX	F.U.
GLOVES	BO/WF + FUF
PATTER	
PIANO	F.U.
REST OF THE WORLD GO BY	DARK COLOURS
DARK DOWN STRUTTERS BALL	BLUES + FUF
PATTER	
POST HORN GALOP	BO/WF + FUF
SAW	COLOURS + FUF
CONCERTINA	DARK COLOURS + FUF

NOTE : LIMES WHITE FOCUS ALL THROUGH

cues are given from the prompt corner: the cue positions are marked on the plot and the board and lime operators take them by listening to the act. It is also assumed that the board operator will listen to and 'feel' the music, so cue timings in seconds are rarely written into the plot.

The traditional variety rehearsal is (or sadly one almost has to say 'was') the Monday band call. On arrival at the theatre, the Acts put their band parts on the footlights to establish a 'first come, first served' rota to have their music rehearsed by the resident musical director (MD), special attention being given to tempi, cues and drummer's effects. While awaiting their turn with the band, the actors unpack their props and confer with the resident stage manager and chief electrician about scenic and lighting requirements. The key document is the running order, showing the times alloted to each act, and the resident stage manager is responsible for ensuring at each performance that the individual acts do not over-run.

When the acts perform in clubs a similar rehearsal routine is obviously required but there is a tendency for the call to be rather more informal and, except in the big clubs, for the staff to be rather less experienced and possibly less professional in their approach.

REVUE

The term *revue* is used to cover a multitude of theatre forms from intimate satire to spectacular diversion. Some forms of revue, compiled from original songs, dances and sketches, are really musicals and are staged as such. The more common form of revue is a mixture of musical and variety. The format is usually a sequence of production scenes interspersed with variety acts. Some of the big spectaculars in places like Las Vegas run for years with regular changes in the featured acts.

In British seaside holiday resorts, the summer revue starring television personalities was, until recently, the standard entertainment. Summer shows are in decline and, with the exception of Blackpool, the average run is now less than 10 weeks. However, the scenery and costumes for the production numbers can be moved each summer to a different town, allowing production costs to be spread over several years. The production numbers are staged with identical techniques to those employed in musicals but with emphasis on visual splendour. Costumes and scenery must appear lavish with the lighting bold, contrasty and colourful. Gauzes must melt away and scenery must move like magic. There is no room for any kind of visual restraint. The acts must be dovetailed into the production so that the joins do not show. Dancers and singers may be used to provide an introduction. Special scenery is often provided for the acts and their music is re-orchestrated to fit the style of the productions's pit band. Each act's red, blue and FUF plot has to be interpreted in terms of the show's lighting rig which is likely to be rather more extensive than the average variety theatre or club. In fact a variety lighting plot contains all the vital information if red and blue are translated as warm and cool, colours interpreted as 'pretty' and full up as meaning bright rather than every single light at full. Blackout usually does mean blackout but blackout with pin focus might just possibly include a touch of backlight or a hint of blue on the cyclorama. The electrics department in a revue usually has to cope, in addition to normal lighting, with all sorts of practicals including star cloths and hundreds of bulbs wired to switch on and off in sequence as 'chasers'.

The main problem in setting and striking – and this is particularly true of summer shows – is musical acts with large drum kits, several keyboards and an assortment of guitar amplifiers. Lengthy front cloth scenes often have to be incorporated into the running order before and after. It helps if most of the gear can be mounted on a truck but many summer theatres have very restricted wing space.

PANTOMIME

The Christmas pantomime is a unique British institution (possibly our only truly indigenous theatre form) and this is certainly not the place to attempt to explain the structure and conventions of its script. It frequently has the technical complexities of a major musical but is rehearsed and staged in a fraction of the time. Pantomime scenery is not quite immortal but it is expected to be still showing considerable life after twenty years or so of annual Christmas seasons. In its declining years it tends to get cut down and may be used for a quite different story subject. As it gets older, increasingly stronger gels are required in the lights to revive its fading charms. The panto pump is primed each year by a couple or so of new shows which start in number one theatres and move outwards, then downwards, to a different theatre each year. The stars not only interpolate their own speciality acts but insert songs, chunks of dialogue, and even complete scenes to suit their own particular talents. Keeping the story line reasonably intact is not easy but it is important as pantomime is often a child's first encounter with the theatre – which also means keeping technical standards very high, although this is not always easy with a long season of twice daily performances.

The biggest single staging problem is keeping the show to its scheduled running time. If a pantomime is found at its first performance to run too long, the number and complexity of scene and costume changes can make cuts incredibly difficult to insert. One cut can introduce a whole sequence of difficulties. Stopwatch timing of every section of dialogue and music is therefore essential. Even the biggest and newest pantos rarely get more than two weeks in the rehearsal room followed by a week on stage, with the standard being a week in the rehearsal room and four days on stage. This means a total of only about twelve hours for technical and dress rehearsals which is very tight for a big musical production full of transformation scenes. However, if the sections are worked on independently – and the structure of a pantomime lends itself to lots of sectional rehearsals going on concurrently – the full rehearsals can be used to polish the joins.

The department needing most organisation may well be props because much of the comedy is visual and the comics are dependent on props, many of which are quite intricate. Because of the short staging time, it is even more true than usual that the show can only be as good as the quality of homework done by the director and production manager.

In fast shows, it is often easier for the stage manager to call the cues from a sequential list rather than from a conventional prompt book.

	ACT I
	WARN LX, TABS, FLYS
	HOUSE TO ½
	CONDUCTOR GO
(FINALE THEME)	HOUSE OUT
	TAPE GO
(TIMP ROLL)	HOUSE TABS OUT
	LX 1
(FAIRY ON)	LX 2
	FLYS 1 (BLACKS)
(BLEED WITH OBOE)	LX 3
	FLYS 2 (GAUZE)
	LX 4
(BOYS LIFT D.L.)	LX 5
	CALL MR THOMPSON
	WARN LX (6—9)
(DAME ENTRANCE)	LX 6
(PATTER)	LX 7
(KIPPER GAG)	LIME TO GREEN
	LIME RESTORE
(INTO NUMBER)	LX 8
(UP TEMPO)	LX 9
	CHECK DRESSER STANDING BY
(FUF)	LX 10
	WARN LX (11—17) FLYS (3+4)
	SMOKE, PS STAR TRAP
(WITCH ON)	LX 11
	FLYS 3
	SMOKE
	TRAP

**STAGE
MANAGING LIGHT
ENTERTAINMENT**

Most light entertainment productions have no bound printed scripts, although pantomimes usually have copies of the dialogue liberally sprinkled with blank spaces for items like 'dame's spot' and 'ghost gag'. A revue prompt copy can and should be made by bringing together such individual scripts as exist for sketches, lyrics, etc. But for running the show it may be better to work from a detailed running order showing all the fly, stage, tab, lighting and effects cues in the sequence that they are given. In any theatre format where there is a lot of ad-libbing, the important line is the tag that triggers the blackout and sets off a whole sequence of cues.

The importance of keeping to time has been indicated and it is customary for the stage manager to log detailed timings of individual sequences in far greater detail than with a play. Any divergence from agreed timings must be brought to the immediate attention of the performer concerned.

15 Staging Tours

Very broadly speaking, there are three types of tour: productions specially staged for touring, prior to London or Broadway try-outs, and normally resident companies presenting a selection of their repertoire.

Tours play in two types of venue: the standard *touring circuit* of theatres whose main product is the touring show and whose staff are accustomed to dealing with its problems, and the *secondary circuit* of miscellaneous halls with small and/or inexperienced staffs. A production specially staged for touring is budgeted and designed to take into account the special circumstances of touring, whereas try-outs and annual tours are special cases. Let us, therefore, start with a consideration of the standard situation of a touring production on the touring circuit.

SCHEDULING THE GET-IN

The standard tour is based on stop-overs in each receiving theatre of one week or, occasionally, multiples of one week. Consequently the total time available for getting out, travelling and getting in to the next date is from Saturday fall of the curtain until its rise on Monday or, for a particularly heavy show, Tuesday. Transport of scenery in Britain is now entirely by road. First, the railways withdrew their traditional free truck concessions for companies travelling their actors by train. Then they could no longer guarantee nationwide delivery by late Sunday or early Monday. And finally the door-to-door convenience of road haulage with its reduction in both wear and tear on the scenery and the labour costs of its handling (loading and unloading are required only at the theatre rather than at both theatre and station as in the old days) brought the theatre–rail connection to an end.

Unless the move is a particularly long distance one such as Aberdeen to Bournemouth, the Sunday get-in can be at 2pm – on many journeys, 9 am is possible. Simple shows, particularly standing set plays, can get in on a Monday but this is tight scheduling and is dependent on the theatres being able to supply enough crew. Touring theatres have small permanent staffs and rely on a pool of part-time casuals for getting the shows in and out at the weekends and working the evening performances if there are scene changes. Many of these casuals have worked every weekend for years and are frequently more experienced than many of the full time theatre technicians. The problem is that many of them are not available during the day on a Monday although some theatres have casual staffs that include workers – often milkmen, postmen or railmen – who can adjust their working hours to be available at tricky times like Monday get-ins and Wednesday matinees. However, as noted in earlier chapters, changing employment patterns have resulted in a pool of casual crew who are available to work virtually full time in theatre without the expectation of full time contracts.

A Monday get-in is attractive because it is cheaper. The details of whether 'them' or 'us' are responsible for payment of staff are defined in the contract, but the general custom is that the theatre pays for a reasonable number of crew to get the show in on a Monday while the touring company pays for the get-out at the end of the week. The cost of any Sunday work is shared equally between theatre and tour. Sunday work, being at double time, is expensive. A common compromise is to work the minimum call of four hours on Sunday. This allows everything to be unloaded, the lighting hung, and the basic set erected. The cost of the Sunday call is often offset by a better deal with the haulage company who like to get their vehicles unloaded on a Sunday and back to base.

Touring theatres are used on many Sundays for concerts and other forms of one night stand performance, and so the only stage work possible is unloading and perhaps some hanging. If the show is particularly heavy, it may be necessary to work overnight after the concert.

TOURING STAFF

The only non-acting staff toured by the simplest plays are the stage management: a stage manager doubling as company manager, a deputy SM to run the corner and at least one ASM (but preferably two) to cope with props and sound effects. As the form of the show grows more complex there is first a touring carpenter and then an electrician added. Musicals normally carry a sound operator. The carpenter and electrician are required only for weekends so it is not unusual for them to go home on Tuesday mornings and reappear on Saturday afternoons.

RESIDENT STAFF CALLS

The touring theatre provides the number of crew requested by the manager of the touring company. There are two different numbers involved: the number of crew required to run the performances and the number required to get the show in. The number to get the show out is always the same as the number to get it in – an old custom now formalised in union agreements. As a result, the touring manager's responsibility for paying the cost of the get-out acts as a brake on the number of crew called for the get-in, even though the theatre picks up the wages bill for the get-in. Judging the ideal number of crew is a finely balanced compromise between too few to do the job efficiently and so many that they get in each other's way. Furthermore, there are few one-theatre towns that can lay on, say, eight experienced casual theatre electricians.

The *staff call* is the touring company's main advance contact with the theatre's backstage staff and is a key link in the formation of a good 'us' and 'them' relationship. The quality of these calls has fallen off in recent years (it is not unknown for the resident stage manager to have to telephone the touring company at the eleventh hour to discover their requirements, even their proposed arrival time).

The main points in calling are:

- Send the call in writing to the resident stage manager and chief electrician at least 10 days in advance.
- The larger the crew required, the longer should be the notice.
- Follow up with a telephone call two or three days before the get-in to check that there are no problems. When there is a touring carpenter and/or electrician, they should make these phone calls to their opposite numbers.
- Never send calls via the theatre manager: they rarely get any further than the front office filing tray.
- Give the time of the call.
- Indicate the likely length of any Sunday calls.
- Give the numbers required in each department for (a) get-in and (b) performance.
- Give the number as 'chief plus' or 'HOD plus' to avoid confusion as to whether head of department is included in the number or not.

COLOUR CALL

If the production is touring a lighting rig or requires any significant alteration to the theatre's standard rig, a plan should be sent at least two weeks in advance. If there is no touring rig, it is advisable to send, with the staff call, a colour call listing the filters required in the theatre's lighting equipment.

PRODUCTION WEEKEND

The first weekend of a tour is rather similar to any other kind of staging weekend except that a Tuesday opening is unlikely. There should be a tech on Sunday evening and a dress rehearsal on Monday afternoon. In the case of the very simplest plays, the Sunday rehearsal may take the form of a run-through in working light. This saves money as the only staffing required is a stand-by electrician. There should not be a Sunday concert on a production weekend but it can happen and this of course wipes out the possibility of a Sunday rehearsal and makes a Tuesday opening inevitable.

Many tours are recast versions of Broadway or London successes using the original scenery and props. The lighting may be simplified so that it can be adapted to use the local equipment wherever possible. Vital extra lights are carried but most British touring theatres now have a sufficient stock of lights to meet the touring needs of most smaller plays. In America it has long been normal to tour a complete lighting rig including dimmer boards. This has now become the practice in Britain for musicals and larger scale plays.

The question of setting line is a little tricky on tour because of variations in apron depth and the space taken up by permanent tormentors, tabs, screens, etc., immediately upstage of the proscenium. One solution is to strike the setting line in relation to the theatre's No. 1 spot bar: it will then be possible to focus the lighting in the same areas each week. But the sightlines in a particular theatre in relation to a particular show always have to be borne in mind. Traditionally this has been a matter for on-the-spot discussion between touring and resident stage managers. New technology, however, has come to the aid of tour planning. Modelbox Ltd in London provide a facility for a production's scenery plans to be checked against the stage plans of all the venues. Since the Modelbox computer files include plans and sightlines for virtually all the theatres on the touring circuit, it is possible to check how a production will fit into each theatre and how the sightlines will be from the worst seats. Once any set modifications have been decided, compromises agreed and flying lines allocated for each theatre, a complete set of plans for the tour can be printed.

An important weekly ritual is the Monday morning visit of the local fire prevention officer who will ask questions about naked flames, pyrotechnic effects, etc., applying a lighter to check the fireproofing of potentially risky materials like gauzes and window curtains. Fire officers' attitudes in tricky circumstances tend to reflect their confidence in the resident stage manager but the fire regulations are on the whole good sound common-sense and no one in their right mind would wish to 'get round' them.

Quite often there will be a carpenter and lighting designer in attendance for the production weekend only: they will put up the set and light it. Whenever possible the touring stage management should watch them like a hawk to see how they do it. However, stage managers are always being called away to the telephone or to sort out prop and wardrobe problems, etc. So they should ensure that proper plans and plots for both scenery and lights are provided and the specialists should talk through these before they leave. During the first week the stage manager should check that all parts of the scenery are correctly and clearly marked, and should have all the spotlights flashed out to see exactly where they have been focused. It is worthwhile having a chat with the resident stage manager about any tricky parts of the fit-up, including the best order in which to carry out certain operations.

CHANGE-OVER
WEEKENDS

After the first week, there are normally no weekend rehearsals: the show is got in, up and lit. The last item, the lighting, should finish by 5pm latest on the Monday but it is not unknown for the last cue to be plotted as the half is being called. Touring theatre staffs are geared to working 'cold' without technical rehearsals but they rely on the touring stage management being particularly calm and clear in their cueing. The success of Monday night depends on gearing the production to the 'art of the possible' and creatively adapting to local conditions.

GET-OUT

The dismantling of the show and loading into transport for the move to the next date is known as the *get-out* (*load out* in America, *bump out* in Australia). Payment of the get-out (i.e. for all work on the show carried out after the fall of the final curtain on Saturday night) is a lump sum per man negotiated in advance by the heads of the theatre's technical departments with the touring manager and based on an estimate of the difficulty of the work and the likely time required to complete it. Traditionally, to ensure that the work was done properly, the get-out was not paid until the loading was completed. However, a combination of the responsibility of modern staffs, the complexity of modern accounting systems, and the requirements of the income tax authorities has brought about a change in such time-hallowed customs. The art of getting out is, not surprisingly, dismantling in the correct order, packing securely, and not leaving anything behind.

GRATUITIES

It is customary for the touring company to show their appreciation for the work of the resident technical staff by making a small disburse-ment. This is often referred to as a 'drink' but normally takes cash form. The small touring companies, travelling without specialist staff, are particularly dependent on the local staff, often beyond the call of contractual duty. In small companies gratuities are disbursed by the touring company manager, in larger ones by the heads of the technical departments. The distribution of the total sum should not be fixed but should vary from week to week to reflect the degree of helpfulness of various individual technicians.

TRY-OUTS

There are two kinds of tours billed as *prior to London*. There are those with a commitment, including finance, for a West End opening on a certain date. And there are those who travel hopefully. The hopeful tours are try-outs in the literal sense: the purpose of touring being to test the show before an audience to find out if it has the potential to become a 'hit', perhaps with re-writing and re-casting. There is not usually enough finance available for a West End run: the hope is that with sufficient evidence of potential success, the necessary backing will be forthcoming. The hopeful tour is now on the decline: this kind of try-out is now more likely to take the form of a three-week run in a regional repertory company. When a hopeful try-out does take to the road, it does so in a way similar to any standard tour.

However, a committed prior-to-London tour is somewhat different. The purpose is to put a final polish on the show by playing to an audience in the evenings while continuing some rehearsal by day. Technically, there is an attempt to reproduce the conditions that will eventually apply in the London theatre and there is much less adaptation to local conditions than with a normal tour. The sets tend to be more complex than normal touring sets and the lighting will, as nearly as possible, be a replica of that to be used in the London theatre. All this requires more staff, more time, more transport, and these add up to more money. In theory some of this extra expenditure should be offset by increased box-office income generated by a glamorously cast new production, but in practice the *prior to* label has been so ill used in the past that regional audiences can be more than a little suspicious until word-of-mouth confirms the worth of the show. As a result, in budgeting such a tour, it is usually necessary to consider some of the touring expenses as production costs rather than running costs: the tour is part of an investment in eventual success.

Unless the production is a play of the very simplest type, the first week should open on a Tuesday. And an overnight get-in immediately following the get-out of the previous week's show is quite frequent. Subsequent weeks may open on a Monday but will need a full Sunday's technical work.

The really big mega-musicals, devised for an international market, have become too complex for trying out on tour, particularly as they often require quite substantial alterations to the fabric of the host theatre. For smaller musicals, there may only be a couple of touring dates, or even just one, and the whole production team is likely to stay with the show for most of the tour as this often involves substitution of new musical numbers and changes in the running order. The changes are often made at short notice and introduce more complications for the technical staff than for the actors. Unsuccessful changes are partially restored – such restorations often being more technically difficult to achieve than making the original cut! Eventually the plots consist mainly of sellotape. It is necessary to 'freeze' the show for the last couple of performances in one date and the first in the next to permit a smooth weekend move.

TOURS BY NATIONAL AND REGIONAL COMPANIES

Many national companies are based on biggish stages, so there is a size problem when they take to the road. Sets need to be adapted and this can be done to some extent by simply leaving out bits. The big opera companies sometimes build simplified versions of their sets using a combination of original and special pieces. Smaller cloths may be required. This is not as expensive a way of mounting a touring production as it sounds (in relation to total costs) because the original costumes and smaller props can be used without modifications and very little rehearsal is required. The touring lighting rig consists of a slightly simplified version of the basic repertoire installation in the home theatre. This lighting will be toured as a complete self-contained rig, controlled through its own board with the cues memorised. In many cases only a few local FOH will be controlled through the theatre's own system.

Such tours, whether drama, opera or dance, usually present a repertoire of up to three or four programmes, the more popular productions being played for perhaps two or three performances during the week with the less popular only once. These companies tour a sizeable staff drawn from their experienced home-based personnel. The success of the operation depends basically on the degree of imaginative skill with which the tour staging staff can adapt to local conditions, trying to follow the spirit rather than the detail of the original production.

SECONDARY TOURING CIRCUIT

This discussion on touring has been assuming a circuit of conventional touring theatres having, as a minimum, a proscenium stage with fly tower and an experienced technical staff of at least five or six plus the possibility of calling upon a pool of experienced casual part-time showmen for evening performances and weekend changeovers.

At the other end of the scale there is the *fit-up tour* which carries everything and assumes nothing. Such a tour does not rely on finding flying space or even a suspension grid above the stage. The company is self-sufficient in that it can mount the show in virtually any kind of building without the assistance of any skilled local staff.

In between, there is a *secondary circuit* consisting mainly of multi-purpose civic halls plus some university theatres and repertory theatres which take in a few weeks of touring between seasons of the resident company. These stages include every possible variation in size, shape and facilities. If they have any common feature, it is a tendency to have very wide proscenium openings coupled with insufficient depth. The staff can be enthusiastic rather than experienced, although occasionally the enthusiasm is tempered by an excess of respect for bureaucratic procedures. There is very rarely a pool of experienced show crew on hand. The lighting equipment has a habit of being inflexible and inaccessible. One cannot depend upon finding either a clear grid or a clear stage: many such things which are taken for granted in the main touring theatre circuit have to be asked for specifically.

If the touring show's technical requirements use anything other than the very basic, an advance 'recce' visit will cover its cost several times over. Any problems tend to be a simple matter of communication and one has to recognise that the big theatre practice of quick phone calls in jargon will not work for unorthodox buildings staffed by enthusiasts who may not have worked anywhere else but have found out how to solve the problems of their own particular stages – if only the touring stage manager will explain the problem.

16   Staging a One Night Stand

Until quite recently it would not have been necessary to devote a chapter to the single performance, known as the *one night stand*: a passing mention at the end of the touring chapter would have been sufficient. However, there has been a rapid growth in the number of Sunday night performances slotted into a theatre's weekly programme. These performances are given on most Sunday nights in touring theatres and during the non-production weekends in drama repertory theatres. Midweek one night stands are given in multi-use civic halls, and touring theatres occasionally offer a week's season of different single night performances.

One night stands do not normally carry scenery and any rehearsing is limited to a short band call and sound balance. A major problem for the host stage can be lack of advance notification of requirements. This is aggravated by the tendency of performers to arrive so close to curtain time that there is a last-minute scramble to complete preparations for the performance and the standard of presentation may suffer as a result.

The casual attitude towards preparing to meet the audience is most obvious with pop groups, although it is sometimes to be found in other stars who have acquired their popular reputation in media outside the live theatre. Pop groups tour extensive sound equipment and their loudspeaker stacks form the scenic surround. The better organised tours carry their own lighting equipment. If the tour includes, as it normally does, venues other than orthodox theatres, the rig will be designed to be free standing without conventional suspension from the flys. A common method is 'genie towers' which raise the rig from stage level by compressed air. The problem for the resident stage staff is often knowing whether a group is going to turn up with equipment or not. Groups have *road managers* (in jargon, *roadies*) but the word 'manager' in this context can be misleading because a roadie's function is often far more concerned with humping equipment than with management.

But the majority of one night stands consist of *An Evening with Miss X* or *Mr Y in Concert*. The star's solo act forms the second part of the evening and before the interval there are supporting acts. If there is an orchestra, it is usually on stage. To cope with all these shows (and the seemingly endless country and western bills that fill the house in many parts of the country) a theatre needs to have a stock staging answer available. If there is an advance call for specific requirements – fine. But if there is no call, then a framework is available to accept most types of performance and give some sort of air of professional presentation.

STAGE SETTING

The basis of the one night stand stage setting is masking drapes in the form of legs, borders and a backdrop. The side masking should be legs, running on and off stage rather than up and down stage to simplify performers' entrances and permit side lighting. If this masking box is made fairly big (i.e. legs in line with the proscenium opening or false proscenium if there is one) it can be narrowed down by flats. In many cases black is the most useful colour for the masking but it can be gloomy for certain types of entertainment. A good solution is to have a series of coloured velour-covered flats which can be set on French braces to shape the acting area and colour it. An optional sky cloth hanging upstage of the black masking is useful for playing colour and the best type is the backlit plastic cloth known as an *Isora*. A *slash* of silver foil strips is useful as an alternative backing. A set of running tabs on a downstage track (in the normal variety theatre 'No 1 runners' position) is essential and it is useful if these tabs are rich but pale-tinted to enable them to accept wide variations in coloured light. Assorted rostra should be available for drum kits, etc., and a couple of small trucks are useful for getting things like guitar amplifiers on and off in a hurry. A set of elegant music stands (with lights) improves the look of an onstage orchestra.

LIGHTING

The lighting requirement is a series of colour washes with some pale lavender or white for comedy and other full-ups. The battens, footlights and floods of the old type stage lighting did this automatically without any adjustments being required to the equipment. Spotlight rigs do the job much more neatly but require focusing. A one night stand rarely has the time or money available for a conventional lighting rehearsal. The quick, effective way to get colour washes is to drop the lighting bars to stage level, colour them exotically and set every lamp to light vertically downwards (this is the one focusing operation that can be done with any certainty when the bar is away from its ultimate dead). When flown out they will give interesting downlight washes without further adjustment – and the light is only on the performers, not splashed all over the masking.

Cross light from stands or towers can add further interest and flexibility in picture composition. The FOH lighting can include pale tints for full-ups plus some saturated colour for the running tabs. The FOH can even be set while they are being coloured, and if necessary when they are all alight: finicky setting of areas is not required, basically it is just a case of soft-edge focus and dropping off the sky cloth. Limes pick out the stars and the stage lighting gives a general but controllable colour ambience. A plastic skycloth is lit from behind by a set of strong colours in a batten or flood bar at the top and a different selection of colours in a groundrow at the bottom. Patterns can be made with spotlights on stands behind the Isora: the translucence of the plastic generally softens everything so again there is a possibility of setting roughly to save time. A great virtue of an Isora is that, since all the light is behind, any object or person in front shows up as a clean silhouette.

Some performers supply variety-style plots, others just say 'Leave it to you'. It can be fun. Especially when a music number has a slow introduction, the operator fades down to a moody light expecting a sad ballad: then suddenly the music goes up tempo without warning. Getting into a bright light smoothly as if it had been plotted that way is a test of anyone's skill in both board operating and instant lighting design.

BUS AND TRUCK   In North America there is a highly developed system of touring musicals for stops as short as one, two or three nights. The show is completely self-contained and even a full musical can fit up in a couple of hours. Europe is begining to learn from these techniques but there is still some way to go.

17 Staging the Amateur Production

There are no really fundamental differences between staging amateur and professional productions. The problem for both is basically one of time. At the final run-through in the rehearsal room, both are (or should be) at exactly the same state of readiness. However, when it comes to integrating the show with the technical apparatus of the stage, the amateur is at a further disadvantage in that, apart from the weekend, all the technical and dress rehearsing has to be accomplished in the evening only. This must be taken into account during planning and will obviously affect the degree of complexity in the staging that can be aimed for.

The average stage facilities available to the amateur company are likely to be less than those taken for granted by the professional; nevertheless, it should be borne in mind that professional companies frequently work (sometimes through necessity, often through choice) with very simple staging. This does not remove the need for organisation: even if the staging consists of a plank and a passion, the plank has to be designed, constructed, transported, set up, lit, and integrated with the passion of the actors.

Therefore, although much of this book is written in terms of the professionally staffed theatre, the areas for decision and the procedures for organisation apply to *all* theatres: specific application to the problems of staging the amateur show is mainly a matter of scale.

BUDGETING

The important point in budgeting is not so much the obvious one that the actors and staff do not get paid, but that the box-office income is restricted by the shortness of the run. The money available for staging will therefore be somewhat limited after such essentials as author's royalties and hire of the hall have been met. But no matter how small the available sum, there should be an agreed proportional allocation between various departments.

SCHEDULING

There is no significant difference in the importance of scheduling or in the basic principles to be observed in allocating the available time.

SCENERY

Unless an amateur company is performing in a professional theatre – a situation more common with operatic societies than dramatic ones – the average stage facilities will be much less than the professional takes for granted. A fly tower is just a dream and even a decent suspension system is a luxury. Wing space tends to be minimal and rented stages often have severe restrictions on making temporary modifications to the standard equipment installation. This installation may be more than merely inadequate – it may well be a positive hindrance. Scenery can rarely come down from the flys and anything going off to the sides probably has to break down into single flats because of the lack of wing space. The most successful answer to the small stage (although not always the most frequently used) is the permanent non-realistic framework with furniture and an occasional representational shape to evoke the location. The answer to the multi-set play is certainly not full-size flats getting entangled with borders and lights in a quick scene change. And if the stage is particularly small and nasty, might it not be better to put some of the audience there and play in the round on the hall floor?

PROPS

Organisation is standard but shortness of run indicates borrowing as the normal means of acquisition.

LIGHTING

The paper planning is still the same whether the show is amateur or professional. There will be less equipment but that is all the more reason for careful planning of the precise use of each instrument: there is no alternative to preparing a lighting rigging plan and a cue synopsis.

SOUND

Playing effects through a domestic tape recorder is trickier than with special decks but if the leaders are clearly marked it can be done – and there are a lot of sound enthusiasts about these days who are willing to have a go at doing it. Reinforcement should only be required for musicals in the biggest halls. Treat hall sound installations with respect, because they may be basically public address systems with a quality more suitable for speech than singing.

WARDROBE

Same organisation required, although some of the actors may be pressed into service to work on their own costumes. But under tactful but strict supervision or there may be some lack of visual ensemble between individual members of the cast.

Many of the most imaginative experimental theatre buildings are to be found in schools, such as this flexible conversion of a former gymnasium at Loretto School in Scotland – shown here in two of its alternative formats. (Architects: Law and Dunbar-Naysmith.)

STAGE MANAGEMENT AND STAFF

Amateur companies are usually like the smaller professional companies where the stage management not only organise but 'do'. There is not usually the same breakdown into specialist departments: everyone mucks in. In some amateur societies the backstage workers, particularly lighting, take their own cues from watching the script and the action rather than from a co-ordinating stage manager. This often introduces problems with cues being mistimed or just plain missed. There is a lot to be said for having a stage manager who gives all the cues.

TECHNICAL AND DRESS REHEARSALS

The success of dress rehearsals in an amateur company depends enormously on the director and stage manager keeping cool and spreading an air of confidence. There is every chance that the company will include one or two inexperienced people unused to the chaos of dress rehearsals. *We* all know that order will ultimately prevail – but *their* confidence needs a boost to see them through. An amateur company is unlikely to be playing in repertoire, but otherwise the procedures are the same with the main problem being not having the day time to sort out problems between consecutive evening dress rehearsals.

AMATEUR SHOW IN A PROFESSIONAL THEATRE

In general, professional theatres enjoy their annual visit from the town's operatic society. It is not just the break from routine. It may be the only week of the year when there is a big company on the stage and a big orchestra in the pit. It is often the theatre's only link with its former glories. For smooth rehearsals and performances it is essential that the society's stage manager familiarise him or herself in advance with that particular theatre's method of cueing. For a clean get-in and fit-up, the key is full advance discussion with the resident stage manager and chief electrician: they are generally very willing to help – remember, most of the theatre staff will have friends and relatives in the chorus.

Glossary

Acting area	The area of the stage setting within which the actor performs.
Apron	Part of the stage projecting towards or into the auditorium. On proscenium stages, the part of the stage in front of the main house curtain.
ASM	Assistant stage manager.
Band call	Any orchestral rehearsal but particularly a musical (i.e. non-acting) rehearsal for performers with orchestra.
Barndoor	Four-flap rotatable shutter which slides into the front colour runners of PC focus spots to shape the beam, and in fresnels both to shape the beam and reduce stray scatter light.
Battens	(1) Lengths of timber at the tops and bottoms of cloths or used to join flats together for flying as a French flat (q.v.). (2) Lengths of overhead flood lighting equipment arranged in three or four alternating circuits for colour mixing.
Beamlight	Lighting instrument with no lens but with a parabolic reflector giving a parallel beam.
Black light	UV (q.v.).
Board	Contraction of 'switchboard' or 'dimmerboard'. The central control point for the stage lighting.
Boom	Vertical pole, usually of scaffolding diameter, for mounting lighting instruments.
Boom arm	Bracket for fixing a lighting instrument to a boom.
Borders	Neutral or designed strips of material hung horizontally over the stage to form a limit to the scene and mask the technical regions above the performance area.
Border lights	American term for battens.
Box set	Naturalistic setting of a complete room built from flats with only the side nearest the audience (the 'fourth wall') missing. Often complete with ceiling.
Brace	Angled support for scenery. The standard adjustable-length brace hooks into a screw-eye on the flat and is either weighted to the floor or attached by a large special large stage screw. See also *French brace*.
Brail	Pulling a flying piece upstage or downstage from its natural free-hanging position by means of short rope lines attached to the ends of the fly bar.

Breast	Pulling a flying piece upstage or downstage from its free-hanging position by means of a rope line passed between the fly floors and crossing the fly bar's suspension lines.
Bridge	(1) An access catwalk passing across the stage or the auditorium ceiling, usually for lighting. (2) Stage floor section which can be raised or lowered.
Build	(1) Constructing a scene from its constituent parts. (2) An increase in light intensity.
Bump out	Australasian term for get-out (q.v.).
Bus and truck	American term for a tour specially designed for short stops (often one, two or three nights).
Call	(1) A notification of a working session (e.g. rehearsal call). (2) A request for actors to come to the stage as their entrance is imminent, formerly by the call boy, now by loudspeaker system in the dressing rooms. (3) An acknowledgment of applause (e.g. curtain call).
Cans	Headsets of earpiece and microphone, used for communications.
Cardioid	A type of directional microphone.
Carousel	Kodak 35mm slide projector with horizontally rotating circular slide magazine.
Casuals	Part time temporary staff.
CCTV	Closed circuit television used to transmit a picture of the stage to backstage and to audience latecomers watching in the foyer. Also used to transmit a picture of the conductor in the pit to the offstage chorus.
Centre line	An imaginary line running from the front of the stage through the exact centre of the proscenium opening.
Chains	Hanging chains are used to suspend battened cloths and borders, also lighting bars, from the hanging bars of a counterweight flying system. Slender chain is sometimes used to weight the bottom of gauzes although electric conduit tubing is usually preferred as it keeps the gauze stretched.
Channel	A sound or lighting control circuit.
Check	Decrease in light intensity.
Circuit	(1) The path from the electrical supply to the lamp. When such a path includes a dimmer, it should be called a channel, but the word 'circuit' is often used loosely to include channel. (2) A Touring Circuit is a series of theatres visited by touring companies.
Cleat	Special piece of shaped timber or metal for tying off rope line – usually in the flys or on the back of scenic flats.
Cloth	Large area of scenic canvas hanging vertically. Top and sides are normally masked. A *backcloth* completes the rear of the scene. A *frontcloth* hangs well downstage usually to hide a scene change taking place behind.
Colour call	Listing of the colour filters required for each lighting instrument.
Counterweights	Weights which are placed in the cradle of a flying system to counterbalance the weight of scenery or lights to be flown.
Cover	Standby or understudy actor, particularly in opera.

Crossfade	Lighting or sound change where some channels increase while others decrease.
CSI	(Compact Source Iodine) A type of high intensity discharge lamp.
Cue	Strictly, the signal that initiates a change of any kind during a performance, but also used to describe what happens on that change.
Cyclorama	Plain cloth extending around and above the stage to give a feeling of infinite space. Term is often used for a blue skycloth, either straight or with a limited curve at the ends.
Dark	A theatre which is temporarily or permanently closed to the public.
Dayman	Permanent full time 'rank and file' member of the staff, e.g. stage dayman, electrics dayman, etc.
Dead	(1) The plotted height of a piece of suspended scenery or masking (*trim* in America). (2) Discarded items of scenery.
Dead lines	Suspension lines which are fixed and not capable of being raised or lowered by the flying system.
Designer	Responsible for conception and supervision of the realisation of the visual aspects of a production. Separate designers may be employed for scenery, costumes and lighting.
Dimmer	Device which controls the amount of electricity passed to a lamp and therefore the intensity of that lamp's brightness.
Dips	Small traps in the stage floor giving acccess to electrical sockets (*floor pockets* in America).
Director	Has the ultimate responsibility for the interpretation of the script through control of the actors and supporting production team.
Discharge lamps	Special high-powered lamps whose use is mostly restricted to follow spots and projection because of difficulties in remote dimming by electrical means.
Dock	(see *Scene dock*)
Double handling	Moving scenery or equipment more than necessary because it was not properly positioned in the first place.
Double purchase	Counterweight flying system where the cradle travels half the distance of the fly bar's travel and therefore leaves the side wall of the stage under the fly galleries clear of flying equipment.
Downstage	The part of the stage nearest to the audience.
Dresser	Helps actors with costume care and costume changing during the performance.
Dress parade	Prior to the first stage dress rehearsal, the actors try wearing each of their costumes in sequence so that the director and designer can check the state of wardrobe readiness.
Drift	The length of suspension wire between the counterweight bar and the top of the piece to be flown.
Electrics	(1) The members of the electrical department. (2) Also all electrical equipment.
Elevator stage	Type of mechanical stage with sections which can be raised or lowered.

Ellipsoidal	Strictly a type of reflector used in many profile spotlights but extended in America as a word to cover all profile spots.
Enclosure	Housing or cabinet containing loudspeaker units.
Equalisation	Series of controls on a sound mixer for adjusting the tonal quality.
Equalisation cut	Switch on the sound mixer to allow equalised tonal quality to be compared with the original non-equalised sound.
False proscenium	A portal (q.v.), particularly one in the downstage area.
False stage	Special stage floor laid for a production to allow trucks, guided by tracks cut into the floor, to be moved by steel wires running in the shallow void between the false and original stage floors.
Feedback	(see *Howlround*)
Fit-up	The initial assembly on the stage of a production's hardware, including the hanging of scenery, building of trucks, etc. Also the installation of production lighting (*electrics fit-up*).
Flash out	Checking whether lights are working by switching them on one at a time.
Flats	Lightweight timber frames covered with scenic canvas. Now often covered with plywood and consequently no longer light in weight.
Floats	Jargon for footlights (q.v.).
Flood	Simple lighting instrument giving a fixed spread of light.
Fly floors	High working platforms at the sides of the stage from which the flying lines are handled.
Flyman	Technician who operates the scenery suspension system above the stage.
Flys	Area above the stage into which scenery can be hoisted out of sight of the audience.
Fly tower	High structure above the stage which contains the flys (q.v.).
Focus	Strictly speaking, the adjustment to give a sharp image but often used to cover the whole process of adjusting the direction and beam of spotlights (in which the desired image may be anything but sharp).
Focus spot	Simple spotlight with lamp and reflector moving together in relation to a PC lens.
FOH	Front-of-house – everything on the audience side of the proscenium, particularly the lighting.
Foldback	Sound reinforcement from backstage loudspeakers to enable actors to hear their musical accompaniment clearly, and to hear their own voices when the sound is heavily reinforced for the audience.
Follow spots	Spotlights with an operator used to follow actors around the stage.
Footlights	Long strip of flooding equipment along the front edge of the stage, arranged in three or four circuits for colour mixing.
Forestage	Area in front of the house curtain on a proscenium stage.
French brace	Timber non-adjustable brace (q.v.) usually attached to a scenic flat by a pin hinge. Often swung flush to the flat on this hinge for packing or flying.

French flat	Scenic flat which is flown into position.
Fresnel spot	Spotlight with soft edges due to fresnel lens which has a stepped moulding on the front and a textured surface on the back.
Front cloth	(1) A cloth (q.v.) hanging at the front of the stage. (2) A variety act which can perform in the shallow depth in front of a front cloth.
Frost	Diffuser filter used to soften the beam from a lighting instrument.
FUF	Full-up-finish. An increase to bright light over the last couple of bars of a musical number.
Fuse	Protective device for an electrical circuit, either a cartridge or piece of special wire which melts when the rated electrical current is exceeded.
Gauze	Fabric with holes which becomes transparent or solid under appropriate lighting conditions (*scrim* in America).
Gels	Jargon for colour filters although they are no longer manufactured from gelatine.
Get-in	Unloading a production into the theatre.
Get-out	Dismantling a production and loading it on to transport for removal from the theatre.
Gobo	A mask placed in the gate of a profile spotlight to shape the beam. It is a simple form of outline projection.
Green	The part of the stage area visible to the audience.
Green room	Room adjacent to the stage (i.e. the green) for the actors to meet and relax.
Grid	The arrangement of wooden or metal slats in which the pulley blocks of the flying system are mounted.
Gridded	Flying piece raised as high as possible into the flys, i.e. to the limit of travel of the set of flying lines.
Groundrow (electrics)	Three- or four-coloured flooding equipment similar to footlights or batten and placed on the stage floor, usually masked by a scenic groundrow.
Groundrow (scenic)	A piece of scenery standing on the stage floor, often only a couple of feet or so high (half a metre or so).
Gun microphones	Very directional microphones for use at longer range – effective at up to about three times the distance of a normal cardioid microphone (q.v.).
Hallkeeper	Stage door keeper.
Hemp	Rope used for flying. The term is used generally to cover all flying systems without counterweights.
Hemp house	Theatre where flying is manual without mechanical advantage from counterweights.
HMI	A type of high intensity discharge lamp used in scenic projectors and follow spots.
HOD	Head of department, particularly a theatre's resident stage manager, master carpenter and chief electrician.
Hook clamp	Clamp for fixing a lighting instrument to a horizontal bar.
Housekeeper	Supervisor of a theatre's cleaning staff.

Houselights	The decorative lighting in the auditorium.
Howlround	High pitched squeal (sometimes called feedback) when a microphone picks up acoustically from a loudspeaker to which it is connected electrically.
Hyper-cardioid	A very directional type of microphone.
Instrument	A lighting unit used for stage lighting such as spotlight or flood. American term but coming into general use. See also *Lamp, Lantern, Luminaire.*
Iris	(1) Adjustable circular diaphragm to alter the gate size in a profile spot. (2) Muscle-operated diaphragm in the human eye which adjusts the eye's aperture to changing light intensities.
Isora	A plastic skycloth, lit from behind.
Jack field	Patching system used mainly in sound where the inputs and outputs are female sockets linked by short cords with male plugs.
Ladder	Framework in the shape of a ladder (but not climbable) for hanging side lighting.
Lamp	The light source within a lighting instrument but sometimes used as an alternative to the words instrument, lantern, spotlight, etc.
Lantern	A lighting instrument.
Legs	Vertical strips of fabric used for masking, either permanent or neutral.
Leko	A manufacturer's brand of ellipsoidal profile spotlight. Use often extended in America to all makes of ellipsoidal.
Lifts	(see *Elevator stage*)
Limes	Jargon for follow spots and their operators.
Line source	A column of loudspeakers mounted vertically in a long slender enclosure (cabinet).
Linnebach	A form of shadow scenic projector.
Load out	American term for get-out (q.v.).
Luminaire	The international word for all kinds of lighting instrument (not just the special instruments used in theatre).
Marking	Placing small discreet marks on the stage floor (temporarily with tape, more permanently with paint) to aid the positioning of scenery and props during a change.
Marking out	Sticking tapes to the rehearsal room floor to indicate the geographical plan of the scenery.
Masking	Neutral material or scenery which defines the performance area and conceals the technical areas.
Master carpenter	(1) Senior member of the scenery staff in the theatre. (2) Senior carpenter in the workshops.
MD	Musical director or conductor.
Mechanist	Alternative term (particularly Australasia) for stage carpenter and stage hand – i.e. technicians responsible for handling scenery on stage.
Memory	Lighting control systems where the intensities of each lamp for each cue are filed automatically in an electronic store.

Mixer	Desk for controlling the quantity, quality and balance of electronically processed sound.
OP	Opposite prompt side of the stage – i.e. stage right (actor's right when facing the audience).
Pan	(1) The directional movement of sound by crossfading from one loudspeaker to another. (2) Movement from side to side of a lighting instrument (as opposed to the up and down movement called *tilt*).
Pan cues	Electronically reproduced sound effects. A term still occasionally but decreasingly used, dating from the time when effects were played on a twin turntable disc machine called a panatrope.
Parcan	A simple lighting instrument utilising a seated beam lamp (par lamp) which produces an almost paralled beam.
Patching	(1) Connecting alternative microphone inputs and loudspeaker outputs. (2) In lighting, originally a frame where dimmers could be connected to appropriate socket outlets but now increasingly a 'soft patch' in the computer which allows any dimmer to be connected to any control channel.
Pc	Plano-convex lens with one surface flat and the other curved. When used in focus spots (q.v.) modern PC lenses have some diffusing texture incorporated in the flat surface, and the PC then refers to prism convex.
Perches	Lighting positions immediately behind the proscenium at each side of the stage. Older theatres had, and some still have, a series of platforms still in these positions.
Perruquier	Specialist in making and/or dressing wigs.
PFL	(Pre-trade Listen) Control on a sound mixer channel which allows the operator to listen in advance to that channel to check that it is working or that the actor is standing by.
Piano dress	Rehearsal with costumes and all technical facilities but using a piano as a substitute for the orchestra so that the director can concentrate on movement and technical problems rather than musical ones.
Pilots	Low intensity or blue lights around the sides of the stage which do not illuminate the acting area but allow actors and technicians to move about safely. See also *Working lights*.
Pin hinge	Hinge with removable pin used to join two pieces of scenery together (one half of the hinge is on each piece of scenery).
Pipe	American term for bar, particularly a bar on which lighting equipment is hung.
Plot	A listing of preparations and actions required during a performance. Each staging department prepares such plots as are required by the individual department's members.
Portal	A framed masking border bolted to framed masking legs and usually given decorative treatment.
Practical	Anything (particularly props and electrics) which has to work realistically rather than merely look realistic.
Preset	Anything which is positioned in advance of its being required – such as props placed on the set before the performance, or a scene set behind a

backcloth, or lighting or sound control desk with facilities to set levels in advance of a cue.

Production manager Responsible for the technical preparation, including budgeting, of new productions.

Profile spot Spotlight which projects a profile or outline of any chosen shape and with any desired degree of hardness/softness of the edges (in America often called leko or ellipsoidal).

Progress shots Sequence of photographs of stage settings and actors used to assist accurate revival of productions.

Prompt book Master copy of the script, containing all actor moves and technical cues, used by the stage management to control the performance.

Props (properties) Furnishings, set-dressings, and all items large and small which cannot be classified as scenery, electrics or wardrobe.

Proscenium theatre The traditional form of theatre where the audience sit in a single block facing the stage and there is a fairly definite division between audience and stage. The position of this division is the *proscenium* and takes many forms from a definite arch, not unlike a picture frame, to an unstressed termination of the auditorium walls and ceiling.

PS Prompt side of the stage – stage left (actor's left when facing the audience).

Pyrotechnics Bombs, bangs, flashes, etc., usually fired electrically.

Reinforcement Increasing the level of sound by electronic amplification.

Repertoire A form of organisation where two or more productions alternate in the course of a week's performance.

Repertory A form of organisation, usually with a permanent company of actors, where each production has a run of limited length. At any time there is normally one production in performance, another in rehearsal, and several in varying degrees of planning.

Repetiteur Pianist and vocal coach in an opera house.

Resident stage manager Title given, mainly in touring theatres, to the master carpenter. Responsible to the theatre manager for the staff and the building, and to the touring manager for provision of performance facilities.

Rifle microphones (see *Gun microphones*)

Ring intercom Communications system linking all technical areas by means of plugging boxes for headset 'cans'.

Riser (1) The vertical part of a step. (2) Microphone which can be raised through a small trap in the stage floor to a convenient height for the actor.

Road manager (roadie) A touring technician with one night stands, particularly pop groups.

Rostrum Portable platform, usually in the form of a collapsible hinged framework with a separate top.

Run Sequence of performances of the same production (as in 'a long run').

Runners Pair of curtains parting at the centre and moving horizontally, particularly those used in the downstage position in variety and revue productions.

Saturation rig	Lighting installation, usually in a repertoire theatre, where the maximum number of spotlights is positioned in every available position.
Scatter	Low-intensity light cast outside the main beam of a spotlight.
Scene dock	High-ceilinged storage adjacent to the stage.
Scrim	American term for gauze (q.v.).
Segue	Musical term for an immediate follow-on. Often used as jargon for any kind of immediate follow-on.
Setting line	A line, usually just upstage of the house curtain and parallel to the front of the stage, from which all positions of scenery are measured.
Showman	Part time member of staff engaged for performances only.
Sightlines	Lines drawn on plan and section to indicate limits of audience vision from extreme seats, including side seats and front and back rows.
Single purchase	Counterweight flying system where the cradle travels the same distance as the fly bar. The counterweight frame therefore occupies the full height of the side wall of the stage.
Sitzprobe	Opera house term for a rehearsal with orchestra where the cast sing but do not act.
Slash	Shiny foil strips hanging from a bar and giving the appearance of a metallic cloth slashed into a series of narrow vertical strips.
Spill	Stray or scatter light outside the main beam of a spotlight.
Spot line	A temporary line dropped from the grid to suspend something in an exact special position.
Sprinklers	Devices which release water automatically in the event of fire.
Staff director	Member of the production team responsible for maintaining the standard of a production in the repertoire, including revivals and cast changes. Usually was the assistant director on the original rehearsals of the production.
Stage director	Formerly the senior member of the stage management team but a title now rarely used in order to avoid confusion with the *director*.
Stage manager	In overall control of the performance with responsibility for signalling the cues that co-ordinate the work of the actors and technicians.
Stagione	Form of repertoire with a very small range of productions in performance at any given time, where each production is given intense rehearsal followed by a burst of performances close together, then placed in store. Each revival is rehearsed almost as if it were a new production.
Standing	Scenery ('standing set') or lights ('standing lights') which do not change during the performance.
Strobe	Device giving a fast series of very short light flashes under which action appears frozen.
Tabs	Originally 'tableaux curtains' which drew outwards and upwards, but now generally applied to any curtain including a vertically flying front curtain (house tabs), and especially a pair of horizontally moving curtains which overlap at the centre and move outwards from that centre.

Tab track	Track with centre overlap for suspending and operating horizontally moving curtains.
Talkback	Two-way communication, usually of the type where one station (e.g. prompt corner) is a master station which can always speak but can choose by a switch whether to listen to any reply.
Tallescope	Alloy vertical ladder on an adjustable wheeled base.
Technical director (administrator/ manager)	Co-ordinates and budgets the work of the technical departments.
Theatre-in-the-round	Form of staging where the audience totally encircle the acting area.
Throw	Distance between a light and the actor or object being lit.
Thrust	Form of stage which projects into the auditorium so that the audience are seated on at least two sides.
Thyristor	Modern electronic device which has become the standard dimmer.
Tilt	Vertical (up/down) movement of a lighting instrument. See also *Pan*.
Topping and tailing	Cutting out dialogue and action between cues in a technical rehearsal.
Tormentors	Narrow masking flats at right angles to the proscenium.
Transformation	Magical scene change where one scene melts into another, often by the use of lights on gauzes/scrims.
Trim	Height above stage level of a hanging piece of scenery or masking. Mainly American (the equivalent in Britain is one of the meanings of *dead*).
Tripe	Several cables from a lighting bar taped together from the end of the bar until the point where they are plugged into the socket outlets of the permanent wiring installation.
Truck	Castored platform on which a scene or part of a scene is built to speed up scene changing.
Tumbling	Flying a cloth from the bottom as well as from the top when there is insufficient height to fly in the normal way.
Tungsten halogen lamps	Special lamps which maintain their initial brightness of light output throughout their life.
Tungsten lamps	Normal lamps whose tungsten filaments gradually lose the brightness of their light output. The stage types are the big brothers of standard domestic lamps.
Upstage	The part of the stage furthest from the audience.
UV	Ultraviolet light (from which harmful radiations have been filtered out) used to light specially treated materials which fluoresce on an otherwise blackened stage.
Video	(see *CCTV*)
Wagon stage	Mechanised stage where the scenery is moved into position on sliding platforms as wide as the proscenium opening and stored in large areas to the sides and rear of the stage.
Wardrobe	General name for the costume department, its staff and the accommodation they occupy.

Wardrobe maintenance	Division of the wardrobe department responsible for the day-to-day cleaning, pressing and running repairs.
Wardrobe plot	Actor-by-actor, scene-by-scene inventory of all the costumes in a production giving a detailed breakdown into every separate item in each costume.
Ways	The number of channels in a lighting control system.
Wings	(1) The technical areas to the sides of the acting area. (2) Scenery standing where the acting area joins those technical areas.
Wipe	Single curtain moving across the stage on a single track (*wipe track*) rather than a pair of curtains on a tab track (q.v.).
Working lights	Stage lights independent from the main dimming system. Switched from the prompt corner but sometimes with an overriding switch in the control room in case the prompt corner forgets to switch them off after a scene change.

Further Reading

STAGE PLANNING	Roderick Ham: *Theatres–Planning Guidance for Design and Adaptation* (Architectural Press, London)
DESIGN	Francis Reid: *Designing for the Theatre* (A & C Black, London; Routledge, New York)
LIGHTING	Richard Pilbrow:*Stage Lighting* (Cassell, London; Drama Book Specialists, New York) Francis Reid: *Discovering Stage Lighting* (Focal Press, London and New York) Francis Reid: *Lighting the Stage* (Focal Press, London and New York) Francis Reid: *The A B C of Stage Lighting* (A & C Black, London; Drama Book Publishers, New York) Francis Reid: *The Stage Lighting Handbook* 4th edition (A & C Black, London; Routledge, New York)
SOUND	David Collison: *Stage Sound* (Cassell, London; Drama Book Specialists, New York) Graham Walne: *Sound for the Theatre* (A & C Black, London)
STAGE MANAGEMENT	Daniel Bond: *Stage Management – A Gentle Art* (A & C Black, London; Routledge, New York)
COSTUME	Jean Hunnisett: *Period Costume for Stage and Screen* (Bell & Hyman, London)
PROPS	Jacqui Gover: *Create Your Own Stage Props* (A & C Black, London)
PRODUCTION DIARY	Jim Hiley: *Theatre at Work – The Diary of the National Theatre's Production of Brecht's Galileo* (Routledge & Kegan Paul, London)
MANAGEMENT	Francis Reid: *Theatre Administration* (A & C Black, London)
EFFECTS	*Effects for the Theatre* ed. Graham Walne (A & C Black, London; Drama Book Publishers, New York)

Index